MW01640340

The Dark Reich

Nazi Secrets, Mysteries, and Occultism:
Historical Facts and Myths

Peter Reinsdyr

Discover more titles from Arkadoz Publishing at

www.arkadoz.com

info@arkadoz.com

ISBN: 9798302556622

TABLE OF CONTENTS

Introduction

Sometimes, reality can be stranger than fiction. It is, therefore, unnecessary to add more fantasies to the genuine historical facts in the field of Nazi occultism, especially when it comes to their weird expeditions and their pseudo-scientific research.

The true amateur of sensational and strange stories can still be fully satisfied with Himmler's Witch Project, the Hollow Earth Theory, or the various moons of the World Ice Theory that fell on our planet and drowned the Atlanteans. This is real history, and some high-ranking Nazis did believe in these theories, no matter how sensational they may sound to modern ears.

It does not add anything to the uncanny spell of such stories to pollute them with material that cannot be verified or, even worse, with pure lies coming straight out of the imagination of poor authors in search of quick money and fame. These made-up stories are usually rewritten in a thousand ways on the Internet, and everyone adds their own personal touch or interpretation, feeding on each other as makeshift sources.

Even if we happen to be dealing with esoteric matters on the fringe of myth and reality, one should not depart from the proper scientific methods that were suggested by Sagan. We should only work on experimental data, observations, and measurements. Facts should be independently confirmed by documented references. Logic should be the basis of all rationale, and every link in the chain of our submitted observations should hold together. One can hypothesize the link between two separate phenomena because they were close in time, place, or shape. However, these still have to be confirmed by some relevant material, such as geographical and physical evidence. Take, for instance, the case of the alleged battles that would have taken place after 1945 in Antarctica between Allied forces and extraordinary Nazi aircraft, looking like UFOs and flying out of underground lairs.

Finally, one should use the rule of Occam's razor: where there are competing hypotheses to explain the same facts, use the simplest, though you may find another one more attractive. The point is not to write a screenplay for a blockbuster but to find out what did happen.

Among many untrue statements, the yet fascinating book *The Morning of the Magicians* written by Pauwels & Bergier in 1960 stresses rightfully that the Nazi era was like a breach in space and time that they called "The Absolute Elsewhere." What happened during these almost 12 years of dictatorship, at the heart of Europe in one of the most civilized and industrially advanced countries, does not match the moral, philosophical, and religious values that prevailed everywhere else at the same time in the world. There is, therefore, a need to revisit all historical facts linked to Nazi "oddities" that one rarely finds in mainstream historians' books.

True occultism did exist in Nazi Germany but was not widespread. It was mainly centered on Himmler's fantasies and his small circle of high-ranking officers. Himmler was, though, the very powerful Reichsführer of the feared SS, and as such, could introduce occult teachings and new religious practices in the training of his elite soldiers as he did, for example, at the Wewelsburg castle. He founded an almost occult and pseudo-scientific institute called the Ahnenerbe that led expeditions as far as Tibet and searched for the Holy Grail in the South of France. Last but not least, Himmler was very much interested in the persecution of witches during the Middle Ages.

Fantasies, urban legends, literary inventions, and pure lies came after the war at the beginning of the '60s. Any book that dealt with Nazis and the occult, Satan, UFOs, or secret treasures was assured to be sold at thousands of copies. Among the purely commercial approach of fake historians and storytellers, there were a few "honest" though fanatic people who managed, by their writings and teachings, to develop a kind of semi-religious version of Nazism that has formed the basis up until today for neo-Nazi movements throughout the world. We shall therefore deal more deeply with such themes as the Black Sun and the Vril force that pervade many of these Nazi New Age creeds.

This book aims to separate historical facts, however esoteric and strange they may be, from post-war fabrications and commercial lies. The amateur of mysteries and dark secrets will not be disappointed, though, since in this quest, reality is often stranger than fiction.

Part One

Secrets of War

Chapter 1

Non-Whites in the German Army

Although Nazism applied racial theories against non-white people, it welcomed volunteers from almost all races in some of its organizations. Non-Germanic soldiers were enlisted in the Wehrmacht as Foreign Volunteers, whereas "Aryan" candidates usually joined the Waffen-SS. Overall, the Waffen-SS and the Foreign Legions combined had around 120 different nationalities representing many races and religions, amounting to approximately 2 million foreign volunteers. In total, around 13 million soldiers, both German and non-German, fought under the Nazi flag during the war. There were even a few American and British volunteer recruits among the POWs.

Jewish Contributions to the Nazi War Effort

According to Bryan Mark Rigg, in his book Hitler's Jewish Soldiers, there were up to 150,000 Jews, or partially Jewish soldiers, in the regular German armed forces. Some of them were even awarded very high decorations, and others became high-ranking officers, like generals and admirals. These Jews considered themselves nonetheless German above all, and not Jews.

Some of these men had been baptized and did not practice Judaism, which offered a modicum of protection. Moreover, they often found themselves forced into combat positions, hoping that loyalty to the German state might save their loved ones. In rare cases, their bravery on the battlefield led to their elevation within the ranks, creating paradoxical situations where Jewish officers led troops in the Nazi war machine.

Field-Marshal Erhard Milch

The most astounding example is Field-Marshal Erhard Milch, who was a "half-Jew" and whose birth certificate was falsified by none other than Goering, who had claimed to Nazi protesters that "I decide who is a Jew and who is an Aryan." There was an exception to the racial laws of Nuremberg, called the concept of *"honorary Aryan."* The whole Japanese people, as well as the Finns, who are not of Indo-European descent, were proclaimed *"honorary Aryans."* Some Jews were considered as such, too, but on a tiny scale, primarily veterans from WWI who won military medals for their bravery during the fights.

Africans and Indians under German Uniform

There were also a few Black people living in Germany at that time. Some were sterilized when Nazis came to power, while the population harshly discriminated against others.

An African Serving in the Free Arabian Legion

Afro-American POW soldiers were usually treated much worse than white American soldiers. Although rare, there have been some confirmed instances of Blacks being enlisted within Nazi organizations, such as the *Hitlerjugend* (Hitler Youth) and the Wehrmacht. There were even a few Blacks in Berlin that were kept in relatively good condition so that they could be used in propaganda movies.

Soldiers of the Free Arabian Legion in Greece, September 1943

The German army also had an influx of volunteers from many nationalities and races. Indians of the *Indische Legion*, for example, served on the Atlantic Wall in France under German uniforms, wearing ethnic insignias of their own, just like Black and Arab soldiers deployed throughout the *Free Arabian Legion* in North Africa.

One particularly intriguing example of collaboration was the involvement of Indian nationalists. Subhas Chandra Bose, an Indian nationalist leader, allied with the Axis powers in hopes of gaining independence from British colonial rule.

Bose formed the *Azad Hind Fauj* (Indian National Army), which included a segment called the *Indische Legion*, under German command.

These Indian soldiers, often Sikh and Hindu, fought under the German flag in Europe, but their goal remained to free India. This collaboration illustrates the complex and sometimes contradictory alliances forged during the war.

A Sikh Soldier from the Indische Legion Controlling French Citizens (1944)

A Patchwork Army Serving the Führer

The idea of a racially pure German army becomes even more questionable when considering the widespread recruitment of foreign volunteers. From Balkan Muslims to Scandinavian nationalists, the ranks of the Waffen-SS turned into a melting pot of diverse ethnic groups and cultural backgrounds, all united under the Nazi banner. Each group had its own unique motivations—some were staunchly anti-communist, others supported the idea of a New European Order under Nazi leadership, some saw an opportunity to fight alongside a powerful ally, while others were simply coerced, such as the French from Alsace, a region annexed by the neighboring Reich.

Among these foreign recruits, the Legion of French Volunteers Against Bolshevism stood out, consisting initially of thousands of French volunteers, including even approximately 200 non-white personnel from French North Africa. These troops were later integrated into the Waffen-SS as the Charlemagne Division and fought fiercely on the Eastern Front, particularly during the Battle of Berlin, where their resilience was noted, though many were killed or captured. The French volunteers saw their fight as a continuation of the battle against communism, which they viewed as a threat to European civilization.

Muslim Soldiers of the SS Handschar Division

Another notable group was the Bosnian Muslim SS divisions, known as the 13th Waffen Mountain Division of the SS Handschar. Formed in 1943, it was composed of Bosnian Muslims who were motivated by a mix of nationalist and religious sentiments. The division was involved in anti-partisan operations in the Balkans, but its record is marred by numerous atrocities against civilians, particularly in Bosnia and Croatia. These dynamics added a complex and paradoxical layer to the German military, yet provided the manpower necessary for the war effort.

Chapter 2

The Spring of Life

The *Lebensborn*, meaning *Spring of Life* in German, was not a breeding organization taking care of Aryan children, as it was claimed after the war. It aimed to lower the very high abortion rate in Germany after WWI (800,000 per year), to take care of orphans during wartime, and to offer social help for children born out of wedlock, whether they were German or not and whether they were in Germany or an occupied country alike. The women, of whom 60 percent were not married, were allowed to give birth anonymously and have their children adopted by Aryan families. The strict conditions for eligibility for the *Lebensborn* benefits followed the Nuremberg racial laws. Therefore, they applied only to members of the so-called Nordic or Aryan race.

The *Lebensborn* played a significant role in the Germanization of abducted Polish children. Approximately 200,000 Polish children, all considered to have "racial value," were forcibly taken from their homes and brought to Germany to be raised by German families in accordance with Nazi ideology. These children underwent harsh screening processes; those who did not meet the so-called Aryan standards were sent to concentration camps, where many faced dire conditions and even death. Those who passed were given new German identities, effectively erasing their past. Similar abductions occurred in other occupied countries, though on a smaller scale. The *Lebensborn* program extended beyond merely caring for children; it was also a clandestine tool used to reshape the demographics of Europe by forcibly assimilating children deemed suitable for the national-socialist vision.

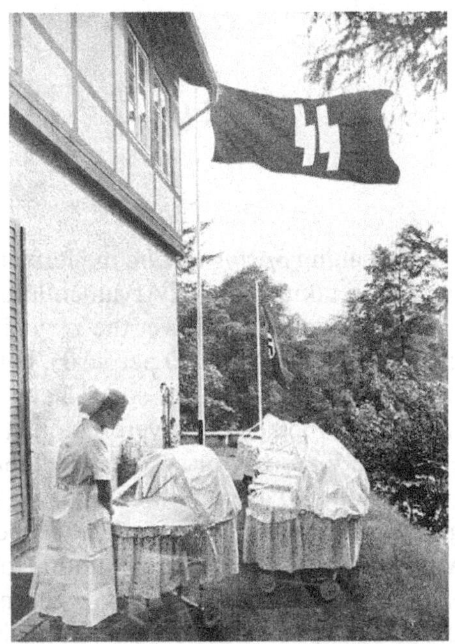

Nurse taking care of Aryan children in a Lebensborn center.

Heinrich Himmler, one of the chief architects of the *Lebensborn*, believed that through careful selection and upbringing, the *Lebensborn* could contribute to creating a master race. Himmler even went as far as to encourage SS officers to father as many children as possible, whether within marriage or out of wedlock, to ensure that the so-called Aryan bloodline flourished.

The Psychological Consequences on the Children

The psychological impact on the children who were adopted through *Lebensborn* was profound. Many of these children grew up not knowing their true heritage, believing they were born German.

Child's baptism according to SS pagan ritual in 1936

After the war, when the truth about *Lebensborn* came to light, many of them experienced severe identity crises. There were cases of individuals, now adults, discovering that their entire childhood had been based on a fabricated identity, leading to lifelong struggles with trauma and questions of belonging.

There were claims of bizarre, esoteric aspects to the *Lebensborn* program. Some historians suggest that the *Lebensborn* homes may have been involved in occult rituals tied to Heinrich Himmler's fascination with mysticism and ancient Germanic beliefs. Himmler was known for his obsession with establishing an SS elite steeped in mysticism, and *Lebensborn* was allegedly part of this larger occult vision. However, these stories—such as secret ceremonies involving astrological dates or rituals meant to ensure the purity of the Aryan bloodline—remain largely anecdotal and lack concrete evidence.

Foreign Women in Lebensborn Facilities

Foreign women from occupied countries were also involved in the *Lebensborn* program. In Norway, for instance, the so-called *Tyskerbarn* (German children) were born to Norwegian women and German soldiers. Norway had one of the highest numbers of *Lebensborn* births, largely due to the Nazi belief that Norwegians were of particularly pure Aryan stock. Himmler himself saw Norway as a crucial area for the breeding of Aryan children, and Norwegian mothers were incentivized to give birth in *Lebensborn* homes, with promises of financial support and better living conditions. The number of such children is estimated to be as high as 12,000.

In France, the children born from relationships between German soldiers and local women faced societal stigma after the war. The *enfants de la guerre* (children of war) were often labeled as "children of the enemy." Many of these children were subjected to severe discrimination and ostracization, particularly during the post-war period when anti-German sentiment was at its peak. This discrimination led to lifelong emotional scars for many of these individuals, who were unfairly punished for circumstances beyond their control. The estimated number of such children in France was around 200,000. Additionally, there were as many as 40,000 in Belgium, 20,000 in the Netherlands, and 4,000 in Finland.

Lebensborn: A Tool for Cultural Erasure

The *Lebensborn* was also used as a tool for cultural erasure. Besides the well-documented abduction of Polish children, lesser-known cases involved the kidnapping of children from Slovenia, Ukraine, and even parts of France. In Slovenia, thousands of children were taken, and only a fraction ever reunited with their families. The Nazi regime aimed to strip these children of their native cultures, languages, and identities, effectively turning them into loyal subjects of the Third Reich. The full extent of these abductions is still not entirely known, as many records were destroyed towards the end of the war.

The *Lebensborn's* legacy is one of immense suffering—not just for the children taken, but for the families left behind, who often never discovered the fate of their loved ones. While officially presented as a benevolent organization, the reality was far more sinister, involving forced abductions and an attempt to engineer the future of Europe through the manipulation of human lives.

Chapter 3

The Nazi Abyss

Lake Toplitz is located in the mountains near Salzburg, Austria. Its shores can be reached only by foot since the only small road close to it is private property. The lake is pretty narrow, only 400 meters wide; it's not that long (2 km) but quite deep (108 m). Because of these particular characteristics, Germans used this site to test their torpedoes.

Towards the end of the war, Nazis wanted to bring Hitler to this natural alpine fortress and organize a last-ditch guerrilla attempt against the Allied troops, which were closing in. However, Hitler committed suicide on April 30, 1945, and this place was used to hide the last secrets of the Third Reich as an absolute last resort to prevent them from falling into Allied hands.

Lake Toplitz's Dark and Deep Waters

During the very last days of WWII, an SS car squad brought mysterious crates close to the lake. Since no vehicle could go further, they knocked at the door of a 21-year-old girl named Ida Weisenbacher, who still lives in a small house close to the lake. "It was five o'clock in the morning; we were still in bed when we heard the knock on the door," remembered Weisenbacher. "'Get up immediately! Hitch up the horse wagon; we need you.'"

She hurried up and guided them to ride their wagon pulled by horses to the lakeshore. "A commander was there. He told us to bring these boxes as fast as possible to Lake Toplitz," added Weisenbacher. The boxes were labeled with bold-painted letters and numbers. She could later testify after carrying three full wagonloads to the lake: "When I brought the last load, I saw how they went to the lake and dropped the boxes into the water. The SS kept shoving me away, but I saw the boxes were sunk into the lake."

Lake Toplitz's dark and deep waters

After the war, many people tried to dive in to find these Nazi treasures, but the odds were low, and the danger was high. The bottom of the lake was carpeted with logs, sometimes standing like an underwater forest made by falling trees from the mountain's steep slopes. In 1947, a US Navy diver became entangled there and drowned. Then, in 1959, a team financed by the German magazine *Stern* managed to retrieve £72 million in forged British currency, hidden in those boxes, together with their money printing press. The fake currency was produced during a secret counterfeiting operation, code-named *Operation Bernhard*, which Adolf Hitler personally authorized to weaken the Allied economies.

In 1963, another diver drowned, and explorations became forbidden until 1983, when a German biologist accidentally discovered more forged British pounds, in addition to numerous Nazi-era rockets that had crashed into the lake. At the turn of the new millennium, other expeditions costing up to US$600,000 were launched in the depths of the lake, one of which brought back some more fake currency. A French company managed to dry some of those soaked banknotes so that they could be shown at an exhibition.

Rumors, Mysteries, and Unconfirmed Allegations

Many speculate that Lake Toplitz may still hide even more significant secrets beneath its murky waters. Some claim that crates of Nazi gold, art treasures, or even secret documents detailing the escape routes of high-ranking Nazis—often referred to as *Ratlines*—might still be hidden under the logs at the bottom of the lake. These stories, though largely anecdotal, have continued to attract treasure hunters from around the world. Local legends also speak of mysterious lights seen at the lake during moonless nights, adding to the aura of mystery that surrounds Lake Toplitz.

Some believe that the lake may have served as a dumping ground for secret weapons prototypes. During a 2000 expedition, researchers discovered several small, unidentified devices buried deep in the silt. Though these were initially thought to be rocket parts, some conspiracy theorists suggest they could be experimental devices for advanced Nazi technology, including early jet or even anti-gravity propulsion systems. The truth about these findings remains elusive, and official records have provided little clarification.

There have also been accounts of divers encountering strange underwater currents and unexplained sonar readings, suggesting the possibility of hidden underwater chambers or tunnels connected to other lakes or mountain locations. These alleged tunnels might have been used by the Nazis to transport valuables in secret, and their existence has never been definitively confirmed or denied.

The SS and Occult Connections

The connection between Lake Toplitz and Nazi occultism is another aspect that has fed the many rumors. Heinrich Himmler, who led the SS and was known for his fascination with mysticism and the occult, was allegedly interested in using the lake as a ritual site. Some reports suggest that the crates sunk in Lake Toplitz contained not just forged money but also occult artifacts, stolen from various locations across Europe. These objects were believed to hold magical power that could protect or curse, depending on the rituals performed. While these accounts lack substantial evidence, the mystique of Nazi occultism has only contributed to the lake's dark allure.

Additionally, anecdotal stories have emerged of strange military activities around Lake Toplitz immediately after the war, allegedly involving both Soviet and American intelligence operatives. These stories, though not verified, suggest that both superpowers were keenly aware of the secrets hidden in the lake and were trying to recover whatever they could. The true extent of these post-war operations remains a mystery, fueling speculation about what might still lie undiscovered in the lake's depths.

Continued Expeditions and Modern Technology

Despite the dangers, attempts to explore Lake Toplitz continue to this day. With advancements in underwater technology, modern expeditions have been able to map the lakebed in far greater detail. In recent years, specialized underwater drones have identified new anomalies beneath the log-covered bottom—metallic masses that some believe could be the remnants of further Nazi activities. The Austrian government has restricted unauthorized diving expeditions, citing safety concerns, but this has not stopped amateur treasure hunters from risking their lives in search of whatever may be hidden below.

In 2018, a high-profile expedition funded by an American millionaire attempted to recover what was rumored to be a Nazi cache of uranium intended for the German nuclear program. While no uranium was found, the expedition did uncover a variety of unusual metallic artifacts, including pieces of what might have been advanced electronics, surprising for their time. These discoveries have led some to speculate about secret Nazi research far beyond what was previously documented, though much of this remains conjecture.

Some claim, with good reason, that there could be more to find there, as any heavy treasure would most likely be hidden under the log forest at the bottom of the lake. The mix of history, rumor, and speculation continues to make Lake Toplitz one of the most enigmatic places tied to the legacy of the Third Reich—a murky abyss where truth and legend coexist, and the search for answers goes on.

Chapter 4

Nazi Werewolves

The name *Werwolf* (German for Werewolf) was initially a novel written by Hermann Löns: *Der Wehrwolf* (1910). This spelling – *Wehr* instead of *Wer* – literally means "the wolf that defends" in German. This book was read by the Free Corps fighters after WWI and held as an example. Some go so far back as to see the *Werwolf*'s origins in the late Middle Ages and the Holy Vehme Courts, a secret society of ordinary citizens taking revenge on criminals who acted negatively towards the community. The criminal was sentenced and often hung on a tree as an advertisement.

Werwolf Insignia on Pennant

By March 1945, when the Final Victory was seen as impossible, Minister of Propaganda Joseph Goebbels fostered the idea of covert guerrilla warfare that would assault the Allies ceaselessly, even after their victory.

The truth is that the *Werwolf* was firstly intended as a uniformed unit and not an intellectual concept of resistance. Though some acts of "terrorism" against enemies of Nazism were accounted for as late as 1948, many put into question whether they were linked to a secret *Werwolf* organization. The only confirmed consequence of the propaganda made around the *Werwolf* was the overestimation of the phenomenon by the Allies, which led to greater hardships for the German population.

Werwolf insignia on pennant

The actual *Werwolf* was initiated by Heinrich Himmler in the summer of 1944 and then entrusted to SS General Hans-Adolf Prützmann. Their recruits, comprising some 5,000 SS men and Hitler Youths alike, were trained with guerrilla tactics similar to those the Germans saw being used by the Soviet partisans in the occupied territories of the East.

The Werwolf Network and Training

On March 23, 1945, Dr. Joseph Goebbels urged every citizen of occupied Germany to act as a *Werwolf*. The movement was intended to create fear among the Allies and to keep German morale high, even in the face of imminent defeat. The recruits were subjected to intense training in sabotage, assassination, and psychological warfare. They were taught how to blend into civilian populations and use everyday objects as weapons—one notable training exercise included making explosives out of household chemicals and using farming tools as makeshift arms.

SS General Prützmann meets with Himmler

Prützmann, the leader of the *Werwolf* operation, had a particular fascination with the tactics used by Soviet partisans, and he sought to emulate their success in tying down German resources. He hoped that the *Werwolf* would have a similar effect on the advancing Allies, turning every village and forest into a potential hotbed of resistance. The *Werwolf* units were provided with hidden caches of weapons, food, and medical supplies to ensure that they could operate independently for extended periods of time.

Infamous Incidents and Acts of Sabotage

Despite the limited success of the *Werwolf*, there were a few incidents that added to their notorious reputation. One of the most famous incidents involved the assassination of Franz Oppenhoff, the newly appointed mayor of Aachen, who was considered too cooperative with the Allies. On March 25, 1945, Oppenhoff was murdered by a *Werwolf* team that had infiltrated the area. This act was one of the few confirmed operations carried out by the *Werwolf* and was intended as a warning to other Germans who considered collaboration.

Another incident involved the derailment of an Allied supply train in Bavaria in April 1945. Though the *Werwolf* fighters were never officially credited with the act, the timing and tactics used were consistent with the type of training they received. In the confusion of the war's final weeks, such actions, even if sporadic, helped cement the *Werwolf*'s image as a force still capable of causing disruption.

Fear and Propaganda: A Psychological Weapon

While the actual impact of the *Werwolf* on the war's outcome was negligible, the psychological impact was far greater. Goebbels' propaganda successfully instilled fear in both the Allies and the German populace. Radio broadcasts and leaflets spread messages urging Germans to resist occupation forces, promising severe consequences for those who collaborated. The threat of *Werwolf* activity was enough to force the Allies to dedicate considerable resources to maintaining control, leading to increased suspicion and harsh retaliatory actions, particularly by Soviet forces.

In the Soviet-occupied zones, paranoia about the *Werwolf* led to the mass detention and execution of German youths, particularly those who were members of the Hitler Youth. Soviet troops, fearful of guerrilla attacks, often reacted brutally, with thousands of suspected *Werwolf* operatives killed without trial. Even unarmed groups of teenagers found wandering the countryside were sometimes summarily executed, reflecting the intense fear that Goebbels' propaganda had managed to instill.

Legacy and the Myth of the Werwolf

The *Werwolf* program ultimately became more of a myth than an effective fighting force. However, its legacy lingered on in post-war Germany. The Allies continued to uncover hidden bunkers and supply caches well into the 1950s, reinforcing the idea that *Werwolf* operatives could still be lying in wait. The mere idea of the *Werwolf* had a profound effect on the way the Allies approached the occupation, leading them to be more heavy-handed in dealing with any suspected insurgency.

Many of the stories surrounding the *Werwolf* have taken on a legendary quality, and the truth is often difficult to separate from the myth. Anecdotal accounts have claimed that even years after the war, isolated attacks on Soviet patrols in the forests of Bavaria and Thuringia were attributed to remnants of the *Werwolf*. These stories, though largely unsubstantiated, contributed to the enduring legend of a hidden, underground resistance movement, ready to strike at any moment.

The Werwolf Concept in Post-War Culture

The concept of the *Werwolf* has since influenced numerous post-war cultural portrayals of Nazi resistance. Books, films, and even video games have depicted the *Werwolf* as a mysterious underground force, ready to rise again. The idea of a secretive, shadowy group of Nazi loyalists hiding in the forests of Germany has captivated the imaginations of many. The movement's association with the supernatural, implied by its name, has further added to its allure, making it a fertile ground for conspiracy theories and popular fiction.

It has been suggested that the *Werwolf* concept may have inspired later insurgent tactics in various global conflicts. The emphasis on blending in with local populations, using rudimentary weapons, and psychological warfare can be seen in numerous guerrilla movements in the latter half of the 20th century. Though the *Werwolf* may have been largely ineffective during WWII, its tactics and the fear it generated were, in some ways, a precursor to modern insurgency tactics.

A Propaganda Masterpiece

In the end, the *Werwolf* was more of a testament to the power of propaganda than to the effectiveness of guerrilla warfare. Dr. Joseph Goebbels succeeded in creating a phantom menace that haunted the minds of the Allies long after the war had ended. The *Werwolf* never became the unified underground movement it was intended to be, but its myth lived on, influencing both the immediate post-war period and the broader cultural imagination. The ghost of the *Werwolf* served as one last reminder of the lengths to which the Nazi regime was willing to go to preserve its ideology, even in the face of inevitable defeat.

Chapter 5

The Underground Reich

In just a few years, Nazi Germany occupied many European countries and managed to introduce noticeable changes in their daily landscape. Some of them are still visible today, such as the bunkers; others are spread underground through extended networks of tunnels and chambers. What was the purpose of such constructions, and did they hide agendas of the strangest kind?

Many know from WWII movies about the impressive chain of bunkers along the Atlantic Wall, which was meant to prevent any attempt of the Allied forces to land by sea. Others may remember pictures of Hitler's headquarters in East Prussia (*Wolfsschanze*, aka *The Wolf's Lair*) or Ukraine (at Vinnitsa: *Werwolf*, aka *The Werewolf*). But who had ever heard of the underground cities in the Jonas Valley or the underground networks of factories at the Dora concentration camp?

They had built no less than fourteen headquarter-ready bunkers for Hitler, of which he actually used ten. Some of them were well known, but others are barely mentioned in the history books. For example, most French are not even aware that a large bunker complex just 60 km from Paris exists in the city of Margival adjacent to Soissons. Except for the people who live very close to it, nobody else had ever visited Hitler's Polish headquarters of Stępina or Strzyżów, referred to as the *Anlage Süd* (Southern Installations). Hitler met Mussolini there on August 27, 1941. Based on the information that I was able to gather from the local elderly personally, villagers were forced to stay put in their homes and asked to close their windows so as not to see the Duce and the Führer while these remained at Stępina.

Stępina Train Bunker, where Mussolini's train was hosted

The same old people told me that just after the war, Polish secret service agents discovered that there was a multi-level structure right under the bunker that may be four to five underground floors. Nobody could know for sure since the Germans flooded the whole building thanks to a nearby river. Polish divers tried to locate the breach in the structure from which the river poured in but always failed. Pumping up the water was, therefore, not an option. Rumors have said that wealthy North Americans of Polish descent will try to invest the necessary money in the near future to stop the leak and drain the bunker and its underground floors. Yet nobody knows precisely what they expect to find down there because of the lack of archives on the matter.

Even more mysterious was the vast network of tunnels and bunkers, which were so big that they sometimes looked like underground cities. Their real purpose has not always been clear to this day.

The less mysterious and yet probably the most gruesome among them was the Dora concentration camp near the city of Nordhausen, with its Mittelwerk factory.

Mittelwerk Factory

The majority of Nazi covert activities took place in their underground facilities beneath Kohnstein Mountain, where they had buried their entire factory that produced the famous V2 rockets. The existence of these rockets was discovered after the Allied air raid on the Peenemünde island's U-boat facilities on August 17 and 18, 1943, which destroyed most of its infrastructure.

Der Riese – The Giant Complex

Der Riese (German for "The Giant") is another pervasive complex of underground tunnels and bunkers in the Owl Mountains and under Książ Castle in Lower Silesia, which was part of Germany then but is now in Poland. It was built in 1943 to serve as another headquarters for Hitler. Its underground bunkers were located in eight different places and took thousands of forced laborers to build.

Kilometers of tunnels are part of the Giant's network.

According to Albert Speer, Minister of Armaments and War Production of the Reich, "These projects required 328,000 cubic yards of reinforced concrete, on top of the masonry involved, and they entailed 277,000 cubic yards of underground passages, 36 miles of roads with six bridges, and 62 miles of pipelines. The 'Giant' complex alone consumed more concrete than what was allocated for the entire population to build their air-raid shelters in 1944." The total cost was almost five times higher than the Wolf's Lair bunker.

The works were never fully completed before the war ended. Since the Polish secret service confiscated the blueprints and all the relevant confidential information, nobody knows its exact purpose to this day. People assume that it was meant to be the biggest of all Hitler's headquarters and a shelter for the underground factories, but this assumption could never be confirmed.

SS General Hans Kammler was in charge of all these underground facilities. Still, since he disappeared in 1945, close to Prague, in Czechoslovakia, his alleged death became surrounded by many controversies, the most likely being that Russian troops shot him in the woods surrounding the Czech capital city. Others claim that he bargained with the US Army to barter his knowledge about German Wonder Weapons in exchange for his immunity in the USA. This theory would not be implausible if he had made it to the Americans before being captured by Soviet troops since Kammler was a man who knew even about the A9 rocket, known as the Amerika rocket, that was going to be built in these 30-meter-high tunnels with the purpose of reaching New York City.

It has been calculated that over half of the underground galleries and chambers have yet to be discovered because an SS team blasted many of their entrances. This is how *The Warsaw Voice* reports what the post-war Polish researchers had estimated: "There are 35 stoneware pipes meant to carry liquid. Where to? We don't know. We measured their depth and tried to use smoke to find out whether the pipes were connected inside and where they ended. We put two lit flares in each opening – the smoke was clearly sucked inside. In one case, we could hear what sounded like an air-lock working. Then we used 26 more flares, and the smoke went inside, but it didn't really come out anywhere. How great must be the capacity of those pipes, or even the underground tunnels, if they could take in such a quantity of smoke!" There seem to be even more tunnels, suggested by the fact that some have been bricked up.

Książ Castle in Poland

Researchers continued claiming, "In some places, pipes come out the surface of the mountain from nowhere, and in others, narrow-gauge railway tracks stick out of piles of rock; such tracks were used to remove the excavated material. There are also empty chambers with no direct connection to the tunnels accessible today or any surface structures. Some elements suggest that the tunnels in the Owl Mountains could have had a multi-level structure, which was seldom seen in other German facilities around the same period. This could confirm the presumption of some amateur explorers that there might still be some things in the corridors that are still inaccessible today. The question of what exactly is involved still remains unanswered. The obvious interest shown in these facilities after the war by the special services either in the Soviet Union, East Germany, or Poland could do nothing to dispel these doubts."

The Nazi Gold Train: A Mysterious Treasure Hunt

In the Owl Mountains, the legend of the Nazi Gold Train has endured for decades. This train, allegedly filled with gold, art treasures, and other valuables looted by the Nazis, was said to have been hidden in a sealed-up rail tunnel or mine in the Central Sudetes by retreating Nazis during the last days of World War II. Despite numerous searches since 1945, including efforts by the Polish Army during the Cold War, no evidence of the train, its tracks, or any treasure has ever been found. Historians generally believe that the train never existed. However, between 2015 and 2018, the legend received renewed global media interest when a Pole and a German claimed to have discovered the train using ground-penetrating radar. The search culminated in an excavation involving the Polish military, state officials, and privately funded individuals. However, the detected anomaly was ultimately found to be a natural geological formation, and no trace of the fabled train was uncovered. Nevertheless, some people continue to believe in its existence, fueled by accounts from locals and wartime records suggesting that a heavily guarded train was indeed seen entering a tunnel, never to be seen again.

The Jonas Valley: The Deep Secrets

The Jonas Valley, or *Jonastal*, in Germany, remains the most mysterious of all underground facilities. The 25 tunnels dug into the mountains were part of a massive construction effort involving tens of thousands of forced laborers. The secrecy was so strict that even today, nobody knows its true purpose. Some suggest it was intended as a secret headquarters for Hitler, while others believe it was a site for testing nuclear weapons or housing factories for producing the Amerika rocket. The entrances to the tunnels were blasted shut after the war, and access remains restricted.

Jonastal: 25 tunnel entrances can be seen entering the mountain

Adding to the intrigue is the claim that the Amber Room, known as the Eighth Wonder of the World, may have been hidden somewhere in these underground labyrinths.

The original Amber Room

The room, a marvel of craftsmanship stolen from Catherine's Palace in Russia, was believed to have been taken by the Germans to Königsberg, where it allegedly disappeared. While many believe it was destroyed, others think it might still be hidden in one of the many sealed-off tunnels of the Jonas Valley.

The Mystery of the Harz Mountains

Last but not least, adventurous minds continue to share stories of hidden treasures in the Harz Mountains. A good friend of mine told me a story passed down from his grandfather, one of the first French soldiers to fight on German soil. He recounted that American soldiers had discovered a deep tunnel, likely in the Harz Mountains. The soldiers were ordered to explore the tunnel, which seemed to stretch endlessly. Allegedly, they came across two dead SS soldiers holding onto MG42 machine guns, apparently trying to prevent anyone from entering further. The American soldiers were then ordered to blast the tunnel shut after 14 kilometers without further exploration. Did the US generals know more than they were letting on, or were they simply afraid of what might be hidden in the depths?

True or not, extraordinary stories continue to be told about the underground Reich. The Nazi legacy beneath the surface remains an enigma—a labyrinth of tunnels, hidden chambers, and lost treasures that still captures the imagination of historians, treasure hunters, and mystery enthusiasts alike.

Chapter 6

Wonder Weapons

The Wonder Weapons (*Wunderwaffen* in German) were cutting-edge weapons and a new means of propaganda in the hands of Dr. Joseph Goebbels. They were technologically so ahead of their time that they gave birth to a whole new myth. Some of them were proven to be quite helpful, like the V2 rockets, while others may have been just as efficient if they had been produced on time and in sufficient quantities to turn the tide of the war around. The most famous example is probably the Me 262 jet engine aircraft; moreover, some Wonder Weapons never developed beyond the stage of blueprints or prototypes.

Many innovative projects were canceled before they even started or were never completed by the time the war ended. We are talking about different types of aircraft carriers, U-boats with all-electric engines using an air-independent propulsion device, which can carry ballistic missiles and super-heavy tanks like the *Ratte* (The Rat), which would have weighed 1,000 metric tons. German scientists had also planned rocket-powered aircraft, reusable A5-type rockets, A11- and A12-type satellite launchers. This *Silbervogel* sub-orbital Amerika bomber could be launched from the mid-Atlantic Azores islands, manned surface-to-air missiles, a sun gun with a concave mirror that could focus reflected sunlight on a specific target on the Earth and possibly destroy an entire city, a gigantic static V-3 cannon to bombard London from their Northern France location, and finally, the infamous German nuclear project.

Silbervogel: Wind tunnel model

The Amerika Bomber Project

The Amerika Bomber Project was a German plan to bomb American soil, especially New York City, thanks to a customized long-range aircraft capable of returning safely back home. The project was eventually abandoned for being too expensive and resource-consuming compared to the relatively small explosive payload it could deliver crossing the Atlantic.

The possibility of dropping a nuclear bomb would have given the project more credit, but it would have taken even more time and resources; the Germans did study nuclear fission and used heavy water from Norway for their experiments, but these researches were spread among so many different administrations that it made it practically impossible for the high command to gather compelling evidence of its feasibility.

In 1955, there was a public allegation that a six-engined Ju 390 aircraft could make such a round-trip drop to New York, as published in the British magazine the *RAF Flying Review* (see chapter about Wonder Weapons). The story was based on "unspecified German aircraft records" that claimed the aircraft had flown over New York City for one hour; it was, however, revised later to a humbler version, which argued that the Ju 390 made a 32-hour reconnaissance flight in late 1944, departing from near Bordeaux (France) and coming as close as 19 km (12 mi) to New York. The pilots allegedly even took pictures of the New York skyline.

After the war ended, aviation historian Dr. Kenneth P. Werrell cast severe doubts on this story, stating that the pictures taken by the pilots had never been found. At a later date, Werrell studied meticulously all available data regarding the Ju 390's range, and he thought that it would have been a most unlikely thing to do.

The final blow to this exciting aviation mystery was given by the German authors Karl Kössler and Günter Ott in their book about the Junker aircraft. Like Werrell, they thought a return flight was not feasible, and they even proved that there never was a flight from which the New York skyline was visible. The reason is simple: France was the "closest" location to fly to America, but the only customized version of the Ju 390 available for such a flight (the Ju 390 V1) was not on French soil at that moment since it was in Prague (Czechoslovakia) from November 1943 until late March 1944.

These German authors offered one more reason why this could not have been done, namely that the Ju 390 V1 prototype was unable to take off with the fuel load necessary for a round-trip flight to America. The second and last model of the Ju 390, Ju 390 V2, was not completed prior to October 1944.

Lethal Gas

The Sarin Gas was discovered in 1938 by two German scientists attempting to create a potent pesticide. In mid-1939, the formula for the agent was passed to the chemical warfare section of the German Army Weapons Office, which ordered that it be brought into mass production for wartime use. Several pilot plants were built, and a high-production facility was still under construction by the time World War II ended. The Nazis initially explored sarin's potential for use in chemical warfare, envisioning it as a decisive weapon capable of incapacitating enemy forces swiftly. Testing revealed its unparalleled lethality, capable of paralyzing targets within minutes, making it ideal for large-scale offensives or defensive operations. However, production challenges, handling risks, storage instability, and Adolf Hitler's aversion to chemical weapons influenced its operational absence. Although sarin could be incorporated into artillery shells, concerns over Allied retaliation, doubts about battlefield effectiveness, and technical hurdles in mass deployment likely deterred its use. Germany's failure to integrate this weapon may have influenced subsequent Cold War chemical weapons development. This gas was later used with devastating effects in a Tokyo subway during the 1995 attack of the Aum Sect.

Type XXI U-Boot

The Type XXI U-Boot, also known as the "Elektroboot," was the first submarine designed to operate primarily submerged rather than as surface ships that could submerge. Unlike previous submarines that spent most of their time on the surface and only submerged when necessary, the Type XXI was intended to remain underwater for the majority of its missions. This revolutionary design provided a significant advantage in escaping detection and launching surprise attacks against Allied vessels.

The Type XXI was equipped with advanced battery systems that allowed it to stay submerged for much longer periods compared to earlier U-boats. By reducing the need to surface frequently, the Type XXI minimized its exposure to Allied aircraft and ships, thus improving its survivability in hostile waters.

Type XXI U-boats in Bergen, Norway

Panzer VIII Maus

The Panzer VIII Maus was completed in late 1944 and was the heaviest tank ever built. The Maus was a super-heavy tank designed by Ferdinand Porsche, weighing nearly 188 metric tons. It was equipped with a 128 mm main gun and a coaxial 75 mm gun, intended to engage both enemy tanks and fortified positions. Despite its formidable armament and thick armor—up to 240 mm in some areas—the Maus was impractical due to its immense weight, which made it difficult to maneuver and almost impossible to transport across bridges. Only two prototypes were ever built, and they saw no combat action. The Maus's design highlighted the limitations of excessive size in tank warfare, particularly regarding logistics and mobility, which ultimately contributed to its limited success.

Panzer VIII Maus with crew members

V-1 Flying Bomb

The V-1 flying bomb (Vergeltungswaffe 1, or Retaliation Weapon 1) was the jet-powered predecessor of modern cruise missiles. Developed by Nazi Germany during World War II, it was designed to target civilian areas, mainly in the United Kingdom. Powered by a pulsejet engine, the V-1 had an effective range of around 250 km and carried an 850 kg warhead. Its distinctive buzzing sound earned it the nickname 'buzz bomb.' The V-1 was launched from various sites across continental Europe, primarily in France and the Netherlands, and it could reach London within 15 minutes of launch. Despite its limitations, such as low speed and basic guidance, the V-1 was a significant step toward developing long-range unmanned weapons. Allied forces developed countermeasures, including fighter intercepts and anti-aircraft guns, to shoot down incoming V-1s, but these weapons nonetheless inflicted significant psychological distress. The technology and concept behind the V-1 heavily influenced future cruise missile development, demonstrating the potential of unmanned, long-range strategic bombing.

V-1 missile on a launch rail at Imperial War Museum, Duxford

The V-2 Rocket

The V-2 rocket, also known as Aggregat-4 or A4, was the world's first long-range guided ballistic missile, developed by Nazi Germany during World War II. It marked a significant advancement in rocketry and was a precursor to modern ballistic missiles and space exploration technology. The V-2 rocket was specifically targeted at London and Antwerp, initiating a new era in warfare that would later influence the Cold War.

The development of the V-2 rocket began in the late 1930s under German engineer Wernher von Braun at the Peenemünde Army Research Center. By 1944, the rocket was ready for deployment, with a liquid-propellant engine enabling it to reach speeds of up to 5,760 kilometers per hour. This allowed it to reach its target in five minutes, making interception nearly impossible. The missile had a range of approximately 320 kilometers, allowing launches from continental Europe to strike major Allied cities.

Unlike the earlier V-1 flying bomb, the V-2 rocket was supersonic and reached the edge of space before descending on its target, making detection extremely difficult. The rocket's speed and altitude marked a technological leap that laid the foundation for post-war rocketry.

V2 rocket

Between September 1944 and March 1945, more than 3,000 V-2 rockets were launched, killing an estimated 9,000 civilians and military personnel. Additionally, around 20,000 concentration camp prisoners and forced laborers died during the production of the V-2 at the Mittelwerk facility. Despite its impact, the V-2 had limited influence on the overall outcome of World War II.

The legacy of the V-2 rocket extended far beyond the war. Both the United States and the Soviet Union captured V-2 rockets and brought German scientists, including Wernher von Braun, to their countries. These scientists played a crucial role in the early space race, leading to the creation of ballistic missiles and space launch vehicles. The V-2 rocket, despite its wartime origins, ultimately became the foundation for space exploration.

Horten Ho 229

The Horten Ho 229, often called the world's first stealth aircraft, was an ambitious project by the Horten brothers, Reimar and Walter, during World War II.

Horten Ho 229

Developed for the German Luftwaffe, this prototype fighter-bomber featured a radical flying-wing design to minimize radar cross-section, presenting a vision of future military aviation.

In 1943, Hermann Göring requested a bomber capable of carrying a 1,000 kg payload over 1,000 kilometers at 1,000 km/h. The Horten brothers responded with a flying-wing design, eliminating the traditional fuselage and tail to reduce drag and radar signature. Though stealth technology was not fully understood at the time, the Ho 229 hinted at future advancements.

Powered by two Junkers Jumo 004B turbojet engines, the Ho 229 reached speeds of up to 977 km/h, making it one of the fastest aircraft of its time. The use of wood in the airframe, due to metal shortages, also helped reduce radar reflectivity, a concept central to later stealth designs.

Only a few prototypes were completed before Germany's defeat in 1945, and the Ho 229 never saw combat. The surviving prototype, the Ho 229 V3, was captured by American forces and shipped to the U.S. as part of Operation Paperclip for examination.

The Horten Ho 229 continues to fascinate aviation enthusiasts and historians. Its design influenced later stealth aircraft, such as the Northrop B-2 Spirit. The Ho 229 was a visionary concept that foreshadowed modern military aviation, leaving a lasting legacy.

The Hummingbird Copter

The Flettner Fl 282 Kolibri ("Hummingbird") was a pioneering helicopter designed during World War II by Anton Flettner, and it holds the distinction of being the first series production helicopter in history. The Fl 282 was a single-seat, open-cockpit, intermeshing-rotor helicopter that utilized an innovative twin-rotor system, eliminating the need for a tail rotor. Its intermeshing rotors provided enhanced stability and control, which made it ideal for naval operations.

Built primarily for reconnaissance and ship-based operations, the Fl 282 was tested extensively by the German Kriegsmarine. Its ability to take off and land on small decks, along with its hovering capabilities, gave it significant tactical advantages for submarine spotting and other surveillance missions. Despite its advanced design, only around 24 units were produced before the end of the war, as Allied bombings disrupted production.

German helicopter Fl 282 Kolibri

The Kolibri represented an early step toward the modern helicopter. Though limited in numbers, it demonstrated the potential of rotorcraft in military roles, foreshadowing the widespread use of helicopters in postwar military aviation.

The Human Bomb

The Fieseler Fi 103R, also known as the Reichenberg, was a manned version of the infamous V-1 flying bomb developed by Nazi Germany during World War II. The Fi 103R was designed to be a piloted weapon, intended for suicide-like attacks where the pilot would almost certainly be killed. Unlike the standard V-1, which was an unmanned missile launched toward targets in Britain, the Reichenberg included a cockpit and controls, allowing a pilot to guide the bomb more precisely to its target.

The Fi 103R was developed in response to a desperate need for more accurate strikes, particularly against high-value military and industrial targets. The Luftwaffe sought volunteers for these missions, and pilots underwent rigorous training with the understanding that their survival was highly unlikely. The intention was for the pilot to bail out shortly before impact, but given the high speeds and instability of the aircraft, the chances of a successful escape were extremely slim.

Fieseler Fi 103R, code-named Reichenberg

Despite several prototypes and test flights, the Fi 103R never saw operational use. By the time it was ready for deployment, the war was turning against Germany, and the effectiveness of such a drastic measure was questioned. The Reichenberg remains a grim symbol of the lengths to which the Nazi regime was willing to go in its increasingly desperate attempts to strike back at the Allies.

The Me 163 Komet

The Messerschmitt Me 163 Komet was a unique, rocket-powered interceptor developed by Nazi Germany during World War II. It holds the distinction of being the only rocket-powered fighter aircraft ever deployed in combat. Designed by Alexander Lippisch, the Me 163 was developed to counter the growing threat of Allied bombers that posed a significant challenge to German defenses.

The Me 163 was capable of remarkable speeds, reaching over 950 km/h (590 mph), which made it the fastest aircraft of its time. It featured a sleek, tailless design and was equipped with a powerful rocket engine that gave it an incredible rate of climb. This allowed it to quickly intercept enemy bomber formations. However, the aircraft's performance came at a cost. The rocket fuel used by the Komet was highly volatile and dangerous, leading to numerous accidents during takeoff, landing, and refueling.

Messerschmitt Me 163

The Komet's operational effectiveness was limited by its extremely short flight time—only about seven minutes of powered flight—and a lack of accuracy in targeting bombers. Once its fuel was depleted, the aircraft had to glide back to base, making it vulnerable to enemy fire. Despite these drawbacks, the Me 163 represented a daring leap in aviation technology. Though it achieved few confirmed kills, the Komet remains a symbol of the innovative but desperate efforts of the German Luftwaffe during the final stages of World War II.

The Jet-Powered Swallow

The Messerschmitt Me 262 Schwalbe ("Swallow") was the world's first operational jet-powered fighter aircraft, developed by Nazi Germany. The Me 262 represented a significant leap in aviation technology, with twin jet engines that allowed it to reach speeds of up to 870 km/h (540 mph), far outpacing any Allied propeller-driven aircraft of its time. Its sleek design and impressive speed made it a formidable weapon in the skies, capable of taking down enemy bombers with devastating effect.

Me 262A at the National Museum of the US Air Force in Dayton

The Me 262 began operational service in 1944, but a combination of factors, including production delays, engine reliability issues, and interference from Nazi leadership, limited its impact. Hitler's insistence on using the Me 262 as a bomber rather than a dedicated fighter delayed its entry into service in an effective role. Despite these setbacks, when properly deployed, the Me 262 was a formidable adversary, demonstrating remarkable capabilities during dogfights and bomber interceptions.

The jet was armed with four 30 mm MK 108 cannons, which made it highly effective against the heavy bombers that were regularly attacking German cities. However, it also faced significant drawbacks, such as mechanical unreliability and vulnerability during takeoff and landing, when the engines were prone to failure. Despite its relatively late deployment and limited numbers, the Me 262 marked the dawn of the jet age and served as a blueprint for future postwar fighter designs.

Heavy Gustav

The Dora, also known as *Schwerer Gustav* ("Gustav" refers to Gustav Krupp, the head of the Krupp company that manufactured this gun), was one of the most massive artillery pieces ever constructed, designed by Nazi Germany during World War II. This ultra-heavy railway gun weighed an astounding 1,350 tons and was capable of firing seven-ton shells over an impressive range of 47 kilometers (29 miles). The gun was developed by Krupp, a prominent German arms manufacturer, and was intended to break through the heavily fortified defenses of the Maginot Line and other enemy fortifications.

The Dora was transported and assembled using railway tracks, taking weeks to set up due to its enormous size and complexity. It required thousands of soldiers to operate and support, making it a logistical challenge. The gun had a barrel length of over 30 meters, and its shells, each the size of a small car, could penetrate up to seven meters of reinforced concrete or even a meter of steel plating. The sheer scale of the gun underscored Germany's commitment to creating "wonder weapons" to compensate for dwindling resources and mounting Allied pressure.

The Dora gun

However, despite its impressive specifications, the Dora was not a game-changer. It was used primarily during the Siege of Sevastopol in 1942, where it destroyed several key fortifications. Ultimately, its practical utility was limited due to its cumbersome deployment process and the evolution of warfare toward more mobile and flexible artillery. The Dora remains a testament to the extreme lengths taken by Nazi Germany in their pursuit of superweapons.

Chapter 7

Supermen and "High" Command

The role of drugs in the Third Reich offers a disturbing glimpse into how chemistry fueled the war machine of Nazi Germany. From the battlefields to the highest echelons of power, substances like methamphetamines, opiates, and a cocktail of other drugs were used to enhance performance, numb pain, and keep a crumbling regime afloat.

Pervitin: The Fuel of the Wehrmacht

Pervitin, a methamphetamine-based drug, was first synthesized in Germany in 1937 by the Temmler pharmaceutical company. Initially marketed as a wonder drug to combat fatigue and depression, Pervitin quickly gained popularity in civilian circles as well as among professionals, including doctors and factory workers, for its stimulant effects. Advertised as a means to increase productivity and enhance mood, it became known as the "housewife's drug" for helping women maintain energy through their demanding routines. However, its effects were particularly suited to the demands of modern warfare, catching the attention of the German military.

By 1939, the Wehrmacht recognized Pervitin's potential to improve soldiers' endurance, focus, and combat efficiency. The drug was soon distributed on a massive scale, nicknamed *Panzer-Schokolade* ("tank chocolate") for tank crews and *Fliegersalz* ("pilot's salt") for the Luftwaffe. Soldiers received Pervitin tablets in their rations, with doses often taken during prolonged operations or grueling marches. It wasn't long before the drug became a staple of the German military's blitzkrieg strategy.

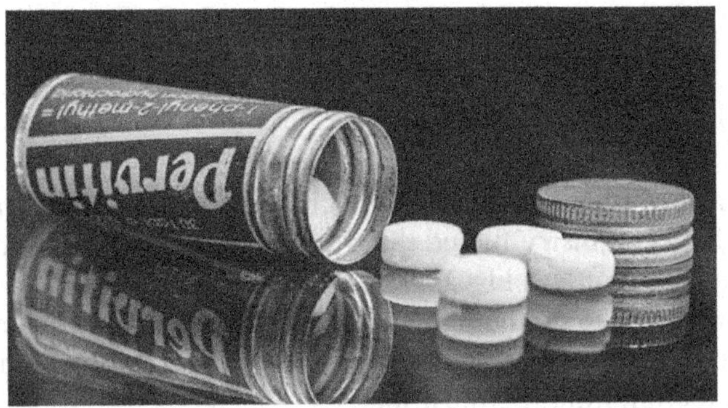

Pervitin

The dramatic effectiveness of Pervitin was first demonstrated during the invasion of Poland in 1939, but its role truly came to prominence during the 1940 Blitzkrieg through France. Panzer divisions, fueled by Pervitin, managed to traverse the Ardennes forest—a terrain deemed impassable by the Allies—and execute an astonishingly rapid advance that outflanked French defenses. German troops marched for up to three days without sleep, covering extraordinary distances and maintaining high levels of coordination and aggression. Letters from Wehrmacht soldiers reveal a euphoric sense of invincibility under Pervitin's influence. One soldier described the drug as providing an "iron will" and erasing fear, making combat feel mechanical and detached. These chemical boosts were integral to the German military's ability to overwhelm France in just six weeks.

However, the side effects of Pervitin soon became apparent. Soldiers began to report severe physical and mental health problems, ranging from exhaustion and dependency to hallucinations, paranoia, and violent outbursts. By 1941, military doctors observed cases of heart failure, strokes, and psychosis among troops who had been consuming the drug regularly. Some soldiers collapsed or became unfit for duty after prolonged use, leading to debates within the Wehrmacht about the costs versus benefits of its distribution. Nevertheless, as the war intensified, Pervitin remained a crucial tool for sustaining troop morale and performance, especially in extreme conditions.

The drug's importance became even more pronounced during the brutal campaigns on the Eastern Front. In the freezing winters of Russia, where temperatures plummeted to -30°C (-22°F), German soldiers endured physical and psychological stresses far beyond ordinary combat. Pervitin was relied upon to stave off exhaustion and despair as soldiers faced relentless Soviet counterattacks, starvation, and exposure. The drug's stimulant effects helped soldiers maintain their focus and push through grueling retreats. However, the crash that followed its use was devastating. Withdrawal symptoms and dependence became widespread, with soldiers often rendered ineffective after the initial burst of energy subsided.

One of the most striking episodes of Pervitin use occurred during Operation Barbarossa, the invasion of the Soviet Union in 1941. The logistical challenges and unrelenting pace of the offensive required troops to stay awake and alert for days on end. Wehrmacht commanders distributed millions of Pervitin tablets to soldiers, emphasizing its role as a "combat multiplier." Some units were known to take doses at such high levels that entire battalions operated in a state of hyperstimulation, appearing unnaturally energetic and aggressive. However, these temporary advantages often came at a long-term cost. Soldiers experienced paranoia, irrational decision-making, and aggression toward comrades. In some cases, psychosis led to acts of extreme cruelty, which have been documented in reports of atrocities committed during this campaign.

Not only did rank-and-file troops consume Pervitin, but higher-ranking officers also relied on it during critical moments. Field Marshal Erwin Rommel, known as the "Desert Fox," allegedly used Pervitin to stay awake and sharp during his high-pressure campaigns in North Africa. This widespread use of the drug underscores how deeply embedded methamphetamine was in the German war machine.

As the war dragged on, German scientists attempted to refine and improve upon Pervitin, even developing experimental stimulants combining methamphetamine with cocaine. These experimental formulations were distributed to select units but proved even more dangerous, often leading to immediate physical collapses and violent breakdowns among test subjects.

By the war's later stages, the adverse effects of Pervitin had become undeniable. Entire units suffered from mass burnout, with soldiers incapacitated by addiction, chronic fatigue, and psychological instability. Some historians argue that the drug's widespread use, while contributing to the Wehrmacht's initial tactical successes, ultimately undermined its operational effectiveness. As Germany's military resources dwindled, the physical toll on its troops compounded the Reich's inability to sustain prolonged combat. Even after the war, veterans struggled with the aftereffects of Pervitin addiction, leaving a shadow over the drug's role in the German war effort.

The story of Pervitin serves as a chilling example of how science and medicine were weaponized during WWII. It reflects the extremes to which the Nazi regime was willing to go to achieve military dominance, often disregarding the long-term consequences for those they sought to exploit in their quest for victory. This methamphetamine-fueled army, once viewed as nearly unstoppable, ultimately became a cautionary tale of the costs of chemical warfare on the human body and mind.

Führer on the Blitz

Adolf Hitler's reliance on pharmacological interventions under the care of his eccentric personal physician, Dr. Theodor Morell, has become a grim symbol of the dysfunction and desperation within the Nazi leadership. Morell, a practitioner of alternative medicine with questionable credentials, gained Hitler's trust in 1936 and prescribed a dizzying array of treatments to sustain the Führer's health and vitality amid the stresses of his dictatorship and wartime leadership. From daily injections of vitamins and hormones to the administration of amphetamines and opioids, Morell's unorthodox methods reveal a troubling chapter in Hitler's life, where science, superstition, and dependency collided with disastrous consequences.

Morell's medical practices were unconventional and often unscientific, reflecting the pseudoscientific undercurrents of the era. He administered treatments ranging from bull testosterone to strychnine-laced tonics, alongside a variety of vitamins and amphetamines. These substances were delivered in regular injections, earning Morell the derisive nickname "Reich Injection Master" among skeptical members of Hitler's inner circle. The medical cocktail included Eukodal, a potent opioid, and Pervitin, a methamphetamine that was widely distributed among German soldiers for its stimulant effects. These drugs, while temporarily energizing, had severe long-term consequences on both Hitler's physical health and mental acuity.

Historical accounts suggest that by the early 1940s, Hitler was taking as many as 28 different substances at any given time. These included experimental treatments with little or no proven efficacy, such as liver extracts, colloidal silver, and even snake venom. The Führer's hypochondria drove him to seek constant medical attention, often compelling Morell to invent new treatments to address his minor ailments. Over the years, the cumulative effects of this toxic treatment plan exacerbated his neurological symptoms, including tremors, erratic mood swings, and paranoia, which became more pronounced as the war turned against Germany.

Dr. Theodor Morell

Hitler's health deteriorated dramatically as the war progressed. By 1944, his trembling hands—a symptom historians often link to Parkinson's disease—were compounded by chronic digestive problems, severe fatigue, and an increasingly gaunt appearance. Morell's interventions did little to address these underlying issues and may have worsened them. Opioids like Eukodal likely masked pain and provided temporary relief, but they also fostered dependency, clouding Hitler's judgment and further isolating him from reality. His infamous micromanagement of military strategies, which many historians attribute to his declining mental state, may have been influenced by the side effects of his drug use.

Morell's treatments also became a source of internal strife within the Nazi leadership. Figures like Heinrich Himmler and Albert Speer viewed the physician with suspicion, accusing him of incompetence or even intentional harm. Himmler, in particular, speculated that Morell's treatment plan was poisoning Hitler, though no direct evidence supports this theory. Despite these concerns, Hitler defended Morell vehemently, crediting him with sustaining his capacity to lead. This loyalty, even as his physical and mental state visibly crumbled, underscores the Führer's increasing dependence on a shrinking circle of advisors and enablers.

As Allied forces closed in on Berlin, Hitler's decline became starkly apparent. Eyewitness accounts from his last days in the Führerbunker describe a man barely recognizable from the charismatic figure who once commanded adoration and fear. Gaunt, stooped, and with hands that shook uncontrollably, Hitler's appearance and behavior shocked those who remained around him. His erratic decisions during this period, including the refusal to allow tactical retreats and his obsession with non-existent reinforcements, reflect a leader detached from reality—likely exacerbated by the effects of Morell's treatment plan.

The final months of Hitler's life also highlight the broader dysfunction within the Nazi leadership. Morell's medical records, seized by Allied forces after the war, provide a detailed account of the substances administered to Hitler, offering a rare glimpse into the intersection of medicine and power during this tumultuous period. These records reveal not only Hitler's addiction to amphetamines and opioids but also his reliance on unproven remedies, driven by a mix of desperation and misplaced trust in Morell's abilities.

Historians continue to debate the extent to which Hitler's drug use influenced his leadership and the course of the war. While some argue that Morell's treatments temporarily sustained Hitler's energy levels, enabling him to endure the demands of his role, others contend that the long-term effects of this toxic treatment plan hastened his physical and mental collapse. By 1945, Hitler's isolation and paranoia had reached a peak, leaving him incapable of rational decision-making as the Third Reich crumbled around him.

The story of Hitler's dependence on Morell's pharmacological concoctions serves as a chilling reminder of the consequences of unchecked power and blind trust in pseudoscience. It also offers a grim reflection of the desperation that permeated the Nazi leadership as their ambitions unraveled. Morell's records remain a macabre yet invaluable resource for understanding the interplay between health, dependency, and leadership during one of history's darkest chapters.

Luftwaffe's High Marshal

While substances like Pervitin and Dr. Theodor Morell's pharmacological concoctions highlight the utilitarian approach to drugs in Nazi Germany, Hermann Göring's addiction tells a different, more personal story of dependency and excess. Göring, the flamboyant commander of the Luftwaffe and a central figure in the Nazi regime, became a morphine addict following injuries sustained during Adolf Hitler's failed Beer Hall Putsch in 1923. Shot in the groin while fleeing, Göring initially relied on the drug for pain management. However, what began as medical necessity spiraled into a relentless addiction that defined his personal and political life.

By the late 1930s, Göring's morphine dependency was no secret among his inner circle. Known for his ostentatious lifestyle, he surrounded himself with opulence, from his palatial Carinhall estate to his lavishly decorated uniforms, dripping with medals and self-awarded honors. His addiction mirrored this excess. As World War II progressed, his morphine use only intensified, exacerbated by his failures as Luftwaffe chief, including the disastrous defeat during the Battle of Britain. Göring's drug dependency likely clouded his judgment, contributing to strategic blunders that hastened the downfall of the Luftwaffe, which he had once proudly built as the world's most powerful air force.

Mugshots from Göring's detention before Nuremberg trials.

When Allied forces captured Göring in May 1945 near Berchtesgaden, they uncovered a stunning hoard of narcotics among his belongings. Stored in a suitcase were over 20,000 pills, including morphine, paracodeine, and sedatives—a pharmaceutical arsenal that painted a stark picture of his addiction. Göring's meticulous documentation of his drug inventory showed a man acutely aware of his dependence, desperate to maintain his supply even as the Third Reich crumbled around him.

At the Nuremberg Trials, Göring's addiction became an object of fascination for his captors and the press. Initially, he underwent a grueling detoxification process under Allied supervision, which stripped him of his drug-induced veneer of composure. Despite the withdrawal, he emerged defiant during the trials, delivering articulate and calculated testimonies. His physical appearance, however, told another story: bloated from years of substance abuse and indulgence, he wore uniforms he had custom-designed to mask his weight gain. These uniforms, absurdly adorned with bright colors and oversized insignias, symbolized both his vanity and his detachment from reality.

The leadership's reliance on drugs like morphine and amphetamines illustrated their growing detachment from reality and their descent into self-destruction. Göring's transformation from a decorated World War I hero to a bloated, drug-addled war criminal encapsulates this decline. His addiction, alongside the broader use of drugs within the Nazi regime, remains a powerful reminder of how the pursuit of power and control often carries a self-destructive cost.

The ultimate irony lies in the unintended consequences of these substances. Designed to build a stronger, more efficient society, they instead hastened the regime's collapse. On the battlefield, drugged soldiers eventually faltered under the strain of addiction and mental deterioration. Within the leadership, figures like Hitler and Göring became increasingly erratic and ineffective. The legacy of Nazi drug use is thus one of profound irony: the same tools meant to secure victory helped sow the seeds of their defeat, leaving a trail of destruction not just across Europe, but within the lives of those who wielded these pharmacological weapons.

Chapter 8

The Nazi Nuclear Research Program

During World War II, Nazi Germany conducted nuclear research with the intent of developing atomic weapons, but their progress was hampered by disjointed efforts and a lack of unified leadership. Unlike the U.S. Manhattan Project, which operated as a well-organized, government-backed initiative, the Nazi nuclear program suffered from competition among different scientific groups, each led by prominent physicists such as Werner Heisenberg, Kurt Diebner, and Walther Bothe. These rivalries, along with inconsistent support from Nazi leadership, kept the program from reaching its full potential.

The Nazi nuclear program, although often dismissed as ultimately unsuccessful, made significant strides in nuclear physics. German scientists had a fundamental understanding of nuclear fission, and Heisenberg and his colleagues laid out theoretical frameworks to create a nuclear reactor. However, the lack of coordination between different research groups, along with conflicting priorities within the Nazi hierarchy, created barriers to true progress. The Nazi leadership, particularly Adolf Hitler, did not grasp the importance of atomic research compared to other "wonder weapons," such as the V-2 rockets. Thus, funding was fragmented and the program never enjoyed the same level of state focus as other armament projects.

Experimental nuclear pile at Haigerloch being disassembled by American and British soldiers in April 1945

One crucial component of Nazi Germany's nuclear ambitions was the effort to obtain heavy water, an essential moderator in nuclear reactors. Heavy water production was concentrated in the Vemork plant in Norway, which became a focal point of Allied intervention during the war. This facility, located in the mountains of Norway, was the only plant in Europe capable of producing heavy water in large quantities. The Allied forces, recognizing the importance of this plant to the German nuclear project, made several daring attempts to sabotage it—a series of missions collectively known as the "heavy water battle."

The "heavy water battle" saw some of the most dramatic resistance efforts of the war. In 1942, British commandos and

Norwegian resistance fighters joined forces in a mission to destroy the plant. Their first attempt was foiled when British gliders carrying the commandos crashed. However, in 1943, a group of Norwegian commandos successfully infiltrated the plant, placing explosives that destroyed key parts of the facility. This sabotage significantly set back German nuclear research. Later that year, the Allies intercepted and destroyed a ferry carrying heavy water that was bound for Germany. These operations not only highlighted the effectiveness of the Allied intelligence but also dealt a severe blow to Nazi efforts to obtain the materials they needed to advance their nuclear ambitions.

Vemork hydroelectric power plant

Despite their setbacks, the Germans managed to create several small experimental nuclear reactors. Werner Heisenberg and his team were working towards achieving critical mass, but due to technical miscalculations, particularly in reactor construction and uranium enrichment, they never reached the point of a sustained nuclear chain reaction. The fragmented nature of the research and the inability to properly fund or unify efforts across different teams ultimately led to the failure of the Nazi atomic bomb project.

The story of Nazi Germany's nuclear research program illustrates a significant contrast to the successful American and Soviet nuclear efforts. While the Nazis had the raw intellectual capability and made some notable advancements in nuclear theory, they lacked the unified strategy, resource allocation, and prioritization that were vital for success. Internal political dynamics, personality conflicts among leading physicists, and Hitler's underestimation of nuclear research all contributed to a disjointed effort that failed to bear fruit.

The heavy water battle remains one of the most iconic episodes of World War II, showcasing the desperate struggle to prevent Nazi Germany from obtaining atomic capabilities. The sabotage missions in Norway not only stymied German progress but also inspired countless acts of bravery and resistance that remain celebrated today. Despite making some remarkable strides, the Nazi nuclear program was ultimately undone by its lack of cohesion and strategic focus—a stark reminder that scientific brilliance alone is insufficient without effective organization and leadership.

Chapter 9

Operation Paperclip

Operation Paperclip was a secret U.S. intelligence initiative that took place at the end of World War II, with the goal of recruiting German scientists, engineers, and technicians who had worked for Nazi Germany. The operation, authorized by President Harry Truman in 1946, sought to harness the technical expertise of these individuals to advance U.S. military and aerospace projects. By bringing over more than 1,600 German experts, including rocket scientists such as those who worked on the V-2 rocket, the U.S. aimed to capitalize on the technological advancements that the Nazi regime had achieved during the war.

The context of Operation Paperclip emerged from the heated rivalry between the Allied powers and the Soviet Union, which would soon evolve into the Cold War. At the time, the U.S. government feared that the Soviets would take advantage of Germany's brightest scientific minds if they were not quickly secured. Therefore, they launched Operation Paperclip to capture the knowledge and ingenuity of these individuals before their expertise could fall into Soviet hands. Among the most famous recruits was a prominent rocket scientist whose work on the V-2 rocket became instrumental in developing the rockets that would eventually propel American astronauts to the moon.

German members of the Von Braun group at NASA

Though these scientists contributed significantly to U.S. military and space achievements, Operation Paperclip was highly controversial. Many of the scientists recruited had been active members of the Nazi Party, and some were directly involved in war crimes, including developing weapons that were used against civilians. To facilitate their entry into the United States, the Joint Intelligence Objectives Agency (JIOA) sometimes manipulated or sanitized the records of these individuals, erasing Nazi affiliations and war crimes from their documents. This sanitization drew criticism, with some pointing out the ethical dilemmas of overlooking atrocities for scientific gain.

The scientists recruited under Operation Paperclip worked in various capacities, ranging from missile development to chemical weapons research. Their involvement was a crucial factor in shaping major U.S. projects, such as the Apollo moon program and the Intercontinental Ballistic Missile (ICBM) program. The presence of former Nazis in such sensitive roles was kept relatively secret from the American public for years, and even when it eventually came to light, it sparked a mix of condemnation and begrudging acknowledgment of their contributions to U.S. achievements.

Test of a Bumper V-2, the first rocket launch from Cape Canaveral.

Operation Paperclip has also been at the heart of several conspiracy theories. Some theories claim that Nazi ideology survived within the American military-industrial complex through these recruits, influencing U.S. policy from within. Others argue that high-ranking Nazi officials used Operation Paperclip as a means to escape justice after World War II.

Although these theories are largely hypothetical, they address the genuine unease many experience regarding the ethical trade-offs involved in technological progress.

The U.S. was not the only country to engage in such recruitment. The Soviet Union launched a similar program known as "Operation Osoaviakhim." In October 1946, the Soviets forcibly relocated over 2,000 German scientists, engineers, and their families to the Soviet Union, where they were tasked with contributing to Soviet missile and aerospace technology. The effort was particularly instrumental in advancing Soviet rocketry, setting the groundwork for the Soviet space program that would later launch Sputnik, the world's first artificial satellite, in 1957.

Likewise, French intelligence also sought to benefit from German expertise, particularly in aviation and rocketry. The French recruitment efforts were less organized compared to those of the U.S. and the Soviets, but French intelligence managed to enlist the help of German scientists to boost France's postwar aeronautical capabilities, contributing significantly to the nation's budding aerospace industry.

The race for German technological expertise after World War II underscores how nations prioritized military and scientific gains over moral considerations during the early stages of the Cold War. Despite the tainted backgrounds of many of the scientists, their work undeniably helped propel both the U.S. and Soviet Union into the space age, leaving a complex legacy that intertwines significant achievements with ethical ambiguity.

Part Two

Nazi Occult Science

Chapter 10

The Thule Society

The Thule Society emerged in the chaotic aftermath of World War I, blending nationalist fervor with esoteric mysticism. Its founder, Rudolf von Sebottendorf, born Rudolf Glauer in 1875 in Hoyerswerda, Germany, led a life steeped in intrigue. After travels in Turkey, he acquired Turkish citizenship and adopted the aristocratic title "Baron von Sebottendorf," likely fabricated. His sudden wealth, shrouded in mystery, may have stemmed from metal trading or shadowy dealings during his time abroad. Influenced by Sufi mysticism and alchemical practices, he claimed to have been initiated into secret knowledge, which profoundly shaped his later activities.

Sebottendorf returned to Germany in 1917, founding the *Germanenorden* (Order of the Germans), a secretive group promoting Aryan mysticism. This group became the foundation for the Thule Society, officially established in Munich in 1918. The name "Thule" referred to a mythical northern land believed by some to be the origin of the Aryan race, echoing themes popularized by earlier esoteric thinkers like Guido von List and Lanz von Liebenfels. Both figures had profound influence on Sebottendorf's ideology: List promoted Aryan mysticism and ancient runes, while Liebenfels fused racial theories with occult practices, envisioning a spiritual mission for the "pure Aryan race."

Activities and Ideology

While the Thule Society presented itself as an esoteric circle, its primary focus was political. It functioned as a nationalist organization opposing the Bolsheviks and promoting Germanic supremacy. Meetings often involved lectures on Aryan mythology, runic symbolism, and pseudo-historical theories glorifying Germanic ancestors. Although rituals inspired by pagan traditions were conducted, these were secondary to the group's political aims.

Emblem of the Thule Society

Sebottendorf envisioned Thule as a bridge between mysticism and action. Its writings emphasized Aryan superiority, aligning with a racial worldview later co-opted by the Nazis. The society attracted around 250 members, including influential figures such as Rudolf Hess, Alfred Rosenberg, and Hans Frank. However, Adolf Hitler was not a member of the Thule Society. Instead, he encountered its ideas indirectly through Karl Harrer, a Thule member who co-founded the Deutsche Arbeiterpartei (DAP), or German Workers' Party, in 1919. This party would evolve into the NSDAP (National Socialist German Workers' Party) under Hitler's leadership, demonstrating Thule's indirect but significant role in the rise of Nazism.

In April 1919, during the brief existence of the Bavarian Soviet Republic, the Thule Society became a hub of anti-Bolshevik activity. Members funded militias, disseminated propaganda, and planned counter-revolutionary actions. However, their resistance drew the attention of Bolshevik authorities. On April 30, 1919, several prominent members were captured and executed in the courtyard of the Bräuninger Hof in Munich. This event galvanized nationalist forces, including the Freikorps, who soon crushed the Soviet Republic.

Occult Practices and Connections

Despite its political focus, the Thule Society maintained an aura of mysticism. Its members dabbled in astrology, divination, and rituals invoking Nordic gods. Sebottendorf himself, influenced by Guido von List and Lanz von Liebenfels, incorporated runic symbolism and esoteric teachings into the society's activities. These elements later inspired Heinrich Himmler, who sought to revive pagan traditions within the SS.

Although Himmler was not formally connected to the Thule Society, he shared its fascination with Aryan mythology. As Reichsführer-SS, he reintroduced pagan rituals and attempted to establish a new Aryan religion. The Ordensburg schools, where SS officers were trained, included teachings on racial purity, Aryan history, and runic magic. At Wewelsburg Castle, Himmler envisioned a spiritual center for the SS, complete with ceremonies venerating Nordic deities and emphasizing their supposed divine mission. Rituals at Wewelsburg reportedly involved oaths sworn on ancient relics and mystical invocations of the Aryan spirit.

Decline and Legacy

After 1919, the Thule Society declined as its members dispersed into other organizations, including the Nazi Party and the SA. Sebottendorf faded from prominence, leaving Germany and briefly resurfacing in the 1930s to publish a book on Thule. By this time, the society's influence had been eclipsed by the more pragmatic and politically focused Nazi movement.

The Thule Society's true legacy lies in its ideological contributions. While its mystical practices are often sensationalized, its racial theories and nationalist propaganda profoundly influenced the Nazis. The synthesis of mythology, mysticism, and politics pioneered by Thule helped shape one of history's most destructive regimes.

Chapter 11

The Hollow Earth

Although this theory is merely a notion that the scientific community dismissed as early as the late 18th century, it still has advocates today.

During the Nazi era, the Hollow Earth Theory had followers in Germany, but not more than in any other Western country during that time. In 1838, Edgar Allan Poe wrote a novel, *The Narrative of Arthur Gordon Pym of Nantucket*, telling us of an awe-inspiring voyage inside the earth by a ship that entered through an alleged hole in the South Pole. In 1871, Edward Bulwer-Lytton published his famous fiction called *The Coming Race*, about some superior creatures, called Vril-ya, that dwelled in the underground world. In 1864, Jules Verne wrote of *A Journey to the Center of the Earth*, where prehistory still existed. In 1922, Ferdinand Ossendowski mentioned in his *Beasts, Men and Gods* the existence of an underground kingdom, with Agarthi as their capital city—the very residence of the King of the World.

The idea of a hidden, underground world fascinated many people throughout the 19th and early 20th centuries. The

Hollow Earth Theory proposed that the Earth was either entirely hollow or had vast subterranean cavities that could sustain life. Some even believed in an inner sun that provided warmth and light to this underground world. This concept was widely popularized through literature and was often tied to the idea of lost civilizations, secret knowledge, and utopian societies.

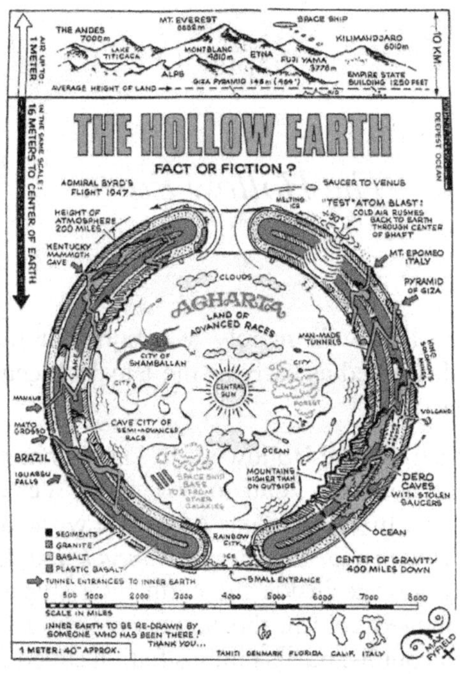

According to the book written by Pauwels & Bergier, *The Morning of the Magicians*, German scientists were allegedly testing life inside a hollow universe on Rugen Island in the Baltic Sea. They even tried to use infrared rays to detect British Navy ships, since the alleged inverted curvature of the Earth would have permitted the monitoring of their whereabouts. This experiment, unsurprisingly, failed miserably and only added to the myth surrounding Nazi pseudo-scientific endeavors.

The Nazi interest in the Hollow Earth Theory was part of their broader focus on unconventional and mystical ideas. While there is no concrete proof that the Nazis officially endorsed the Hollow Earth Theory, it is plausible that some individuals within the regime were intrigued by the concept due to their general obsession with the occult.

The only proven link with the Nazis is their fondness for tunnels, including underground bases and bunkers, that sometimes stretched for hundreds of kilometers, like those close to the Dora concentration camp in the Harz Mountains of Germany or in the vast complex called Der Riese (The Giant) in what today is southwestern Poland. These extensive underground projects were primarily built for strategic purposes, such as protecting critical war production from Allied bombings. However, their existence has often fueled speculation about secret underground cities and hidden Nazi projects, further intertwining with the myths of the Hollow Earth.

One notable proponent of the Hollow Earth Theory during the 20th century was Karl Neupert, a German author who wrote about the concept of a subterranean world and claimed that various governments were hiding the truth from the public. Neupert formulated his theory before 1945, contributing to the mystical narratives that gained traction during the interwar period. His work added to the mystique and continued the legacy of earlier authors like Bulwer-Lytton and Jules Verne, who had inspired generations of readers to ponder the possibility of hidden worlds beneath our feet. Neupert's writings, although largely dismissed by mainstream science, found a niche audience and contributed to the enduring fascination with the Hollow Earth.

The theory also inspired a number of conspiracy theories post-World War II, with claims that the Nazis had escaped to an underground haven at the poles or had discovered entry points to a subterranean world. These stories persisted, particularly during the Cold War, as they fed into broader fears of secret Nazi bases and advanced technologies hidden from the public eye. While these ideas are far-fetched, they underscore how deeply the concept of a Hollow Earth had permeated popular culture.

Chapter 12

The World Ice Theory

The World Ice Theory (WEL or *Welteislehre* in German) is a cosmological theory that originated with Hanns Hörbiger, an Austrian mechanical engineer whose daily work was far from astronomy. Hörbiger's theory proposed that ice was the fundamental element driving cosmic events and shaping the universe. According to him, ice was not just an incidental material but a central force that influenced the formation of stars, planets, and even human civilization. Hörbiger's ideas, although lacking any scientific basis, managed to gain some traction in early 20th-century Europe, particularly during the Nazi era.

Hörbiger claimed that he gained knowledge of this theory from "visions" he experienced while sleeping around 1894. These dreams, he believed, revealed cosmic truths about the nature of ice and its significance in shaping the universe. According to the World Ice Theory, massive blocks of ice influenced the Earth's formation, and large "ice moons" periodically fell onto the planet, causing cataclysmic events. These events, Hörbiger asserted, wiped out entire ancient civilizations, including the fabled Atlantis. He further believed that ice played a role in the cycles of extinction and renewal of life on Earth, tying the theory to myths and legends that have captivated humanity for centuries.

Hanns Hörbiger (1860 – 1931)

Hörbiger's World Ice Theory postulated that ice is omnipresent in the universe, affecting celestial bodies and even our solar system. He argued that our moon was an icy body that would eventually crash into the Earth, triggering a global catastrophe. Similarly, he claimed that past collisions of ice moons were responsible for major geological transformations and mass extinctions. Hörbiger's theory borrowed heavily from myths, blending scientific-sounding claims with folklore to give it an air of legitimacy. Despite its pseudo-scientific nature, the WEL found a receptive audience among those fascinated by esoteric and alternative theories.

Himmler and Hitler were initially enthusiastic about the World Ice Theory due to its purported potential for weather forecasting and its alignment with Nazi ideological goals. The Führer went so far as to adopt it as the Nazi Party's official cosmology, believing that it supported the superiority of the Aryan race by connecting their ancestry to cosmic forces. The WEL also provided an alternative narrative to mainstream science, which the Nazis often labeled as "Jewish science." This was consistent with their broader rejection of established scientific theories, including Einstein's theory of relativity.

Himmler, who had a deep fascination with occult and mystical ideas, encouraged the promotion of the World Ice Theory. The *Ahnenerbe*, the Nazi organization dedicated to researching Aryan heritage, was tasked with investigating the theory's potential applications. It was hoped that the WEL could offer practical benefits, such as improved weather prediction, which would be advantageous for military campaigns. However, despite initial support, the lack of empirical evidence and the theory's failure to provide reliable forecasts led to a decline in official enthusiasm.

Eventually, the Propaganda Ministry, under Joseph Goebbels, ordered Hörbiger to cease all related publications. The theory was increasingly seen as an embarrassment to the Nazi leadership, who began to prioritize more scientifically credible research that could provide tangible military advantages. By the end of World War II, the World Ice Theory had largely faded into obscurity, surviving only among some minor Nazi circles who continued to cling to its mystical aspects as part of their ideology.

The World Ice Theory did not survive World War II, except in the fringes of neo-Nazi and esoteric circles. After the war, Hörbiger's ideas were largely discredited, and mainstream science dismissed them as unfounded. Nevertheless, the theory had a lasting cultural impact, as it highlighted the extent to which pseudoscience could be weaponized by authoritarian regimes to promote their ideologies. The WEL served as an example of how political interests could influence scientific inquiry, favoring fantastical ideas over rational thought.

Despite its lack of scientific merit, the World Ice Theory continues to hold a place in the annals of fringe science. Its appeal lay in its grand narrative that connected the cosmos to human history, offering an alternative worldview that defied established scientific principles.

Chapter 13

Nazi UFOs in Antarctica

New Swabia (*Neuschwabenland* in German, Swabia being a province) is the region of Antarctica under Norwegian influence. It is named after the boat *Schwabenland* of the German Antarctic Expedition of 1938- 1939. This boat could carry and catapult two aircraft.

Before 1938, two German expeditions attempted to cross Antarctica: the Gauss expedition from 1901 to 1903 and the Filchner expedition from 1911 to 1912. Germany decided in 1937 to put a whaling fleet to sea for economic reasons. After successfully returning home to Nazi Germany, which was in dire need of whale fat for its industry, they launched their infamous 1938-1939 expedition. Their hidden agenda was to find a good location for a German naval base.

Because of the initial lack of information and the secrecy of the operation, conspiracy theories emerged about the Nazi survival bases under the ice in New Swabia and their subsequent destruction by the British and American troops (the notorious High Jump Operation led by Admiral Byrd). One enigmatic clue comes from two statements made by Admiral Dönitz, first after the expedition returned in 1939 and then later in 1944; he allegedly claimed, "My U-boat operators discovered a real earthly paradise" and then that "Germany's submarine fleet is proud that it created an unassailable fortress for the Führer on the other end of the world.

The Schwabenland ship

During the Nuremberg Trials, Dönitz would have spoken of "an invisible fortification amid that eternal ice."

Once more, we have to deal with post-war fantasies, as Colin Summerhayes very accurately debunks this in his serious and well-researched article called *Hitler's Antarctic Base: The Myth and the Reality*, first published in the *Polar Record Magazine*, issue 43, of the Cambridge University Press (2007). He concludes that "Using background knowledge of Antarctica, and information concerning these activities that have been published since the early 1940s, it is now demonstrated that the two U-boats U-530 and U-977 could not have reached Antarctica; that there was no secret wartime German base in Dronning Maud Land; that SAS troops did not attack the alleged German base; that the SAS men in the region had civilian jobs at the time; that Operation Highjump was designed to train the US Navy for a possible war with the Soviet Union in the Arctic, the reason why not to attack an alleged German base in Antarctica; and that Operation Argus took place over the ocean more than 2,000 km north of Dronning Maud Land. Activities that were classified have subsequently been declassified, and it is no longer difficult to separate fact from fancy, even though many may find it fancy not to do so."

Furthermore, there is the famous myth surrounding U-530 and U-977, two German submarines that surrendered at Mar del Plata (Argentina) weeks after the end of the war. If we are to believe cheap books on that matter, these U-boats carried none less than Hitler and Eva Braun to an Antarctica underground lair with plenty of supplies to prepare for the advent of the Fourth Reich or the construction of UFOs. Once more, let's refer to Colin Summerhayes' scientific approach that states clearly:

"Consideration of dates, times, and speeds suggests that neither U-530 nor U-977 had time to visit Antarctica. But sailors can lie, and ship's logs can be forged. The question we ask here is: was such a visit physically possible under the conditions prevailing at the time?

All previous considerations have omitted to note that June, July, and August are mid-winter months in the southern hemisphere. Could a submarine reach the coast of Dronning Maud Land, surface, and unload onto the ice shelf mid-winter? The first obstacle would be the notorious Southern Ocean itself. The second obstacle would be the pack ice 1-2 m thick that surrounds Antarctica during the winter. Satellite data collected by NASA (Gloersen and others 1992) and by India (Vyas and others 2004) show that off Dronning Maud Land, the pack ice extends around 500km out from the coast in late May and June and 1,665 km from the coast in July, August, and September [...]

Could U-boats surface through 1–2m of pack ice?

Because of their low freeboard, World War II submarines could easily be damaged by pack ice. […]

Supposing that U-977 had reached the coast, what circumstances would have met the crew?

The 24-hour darkness and the cloud cover would vastly increase the danger of navigating in ice close to a poorly mapped coast. Even seeing the 'coast' would have been difficult because it comprises the 10-30 m high ice cliff at the edge of the ice shelf, which would be more or less invisible in the dark from the low deck of a submarine, not forgetting that the icy seas would be strewn with icebergs […]. [It] means that it would have been physically impossible for U-530 or U-977 to have gone anywhere near the coast of Antarctica in June, July, or August 1945.

Official insignia of the 1938-1939 expedition

[Even if that had been possible] anyone landing from a submarine would have faced the most extraordinary difficulties in trekking 250 km across ice penetrated by hidden crevasses, in the dark and without navigational aids to a lair in the mountains where the temperatures would have been lower, down to -50∘C (Ohta 1999) and the weather worse."

People who still hesitate should read this article in full, easily found on Internet, since it proves in detail that all that was written before were pure fantasies, if not even gross lies. A scientific approach is always preferable to an unsubstantiated claim based on "anonymous insiders" and "government conspiracies."

Chapter 14

Nazi Expeditions

In 1935, Himmler met with racial experts and founded an organization called *Deutsches Ahnenerbe, Studiengesellschaft für Geistesurgeschichte* ("German Ancestral Heritage, Society for the Study of the History of Primeval Ideas"). In short, it was just called the Ahnenerbe. The most prominent and final chief of the organization was Wolfram Sievers, who was condemned to death at the Nuremberg Trials.

The goal of the Ahnenerbe was to study and research the ethnological, anthropological, and cultural history of the Nordic race, the so-called Aryan race. They organized expeditions in different parts of the world to search for the birthplace of the Aryan race and proof that it once ruled the world. The outbreak of WWII put an almost complete end to all faraway expeditions.

The Ahnenerbe had different departments, and although most of them were dedicated to archeology, they also had a meteorological section based on Hanns Hörbiger's World Ice Theory and a musicology section.

The official insignia of the Ahnenerbe

The Ahnenerbe's expeditions were numerous:

Karelia, Finland (1935): The goal was to record old sorcerers' and witches' chants, which were supposed to contain remnants of ancient Aryan pagan incantations.

Bohuslän, Sweden (1936): The team set off to the country's most ancient rock art site, where ideograms were carved. Wirth, the then-president of the Ahnenerbe, tried to prove that he had found a prehistoric alphabet among these petroglyphs but used a less-than-rigorous scientific method.

Italy (1937) and ***Middle East*** (1938): Two researchers, Franz Altheim and Erika Trautmann, went to Italy and then to Romania, Turkey, Greece, Lebanon, Syria, and Iraq to prove that the Roman Empire's success was due to its Aryan racial base.

Germany (1937-1938): Researchers excavated ancient fortresses and found prehistoric caves with Cro-Magnon artifacts. Some other SS studied the famous Extern Steine, which would hold the proof about advanced Germanic prehistoric tribes with a highly organized and sophisticated solar religion.

France: The same researchers visited well-known prehistoric caves in France. Furthermore, during the war, the SS tried to steal the Bayeux Tapestry (showing the Norman invasion of England) since this would have proven the superiority of the Germanic tribes.

The most mysterious case is that of Otto Rahn, an SS sent as a civilian to southwestern France pre-war to look for the Holy Grail, allegedly kept by the Cathars of Montségur. Rahn wrote interesting books about these legends. The strange part is that he died, literally frozen to death in the mountains, once he was back in Germany. Some suspect that it could have been neither an accident nor a suicide.

Spain: a recent archaeological exhibition in Bremen (Germany), "*Dig for Germania. Archaeology under the Swastika,*" shows how the Nazis launched an expedition during WWII to find the Holy Grail. The truth turns out to be stranger than fiction. The exhibition tells how SS Reichsführer Heinrich Himmler allegedly visited Spain because he believed the grail was at the Montserrat Abbey near Barcelona.

He believed that finding the grail "would help Germany win the war and give him supernatural powers." Many undercover SS scientists searched in vain for the grail. The SS budget for such projects was vast inside the Ahnenerbe as the Nazis intended their finds to rewrite history and prove Germans to be the master race.

Tibet (1938-1939): Much has been said about this expedition. It would have had an esoteric and occult agenda to establish contacts with Bon Pö monks, who practiced shamanic black magic, enabling the Nazis to win the war. The only element of truth is that Himmler was very enthusiastic about Asian mysticism and wished to recruit "true Ahnenerbe scientists" like Edmund Kiss to test Hanns Hörbiger's World Ice Theory in Tibet.

As stated by Ernst Schäfer in a 1994 Italian documentary called *Il Nazismo Esoterico*, the truth is far less mystic than all the fantasies that flood the Internet with conspiracy theories. Schäfer stated clearly that there was nothing occult in this expedition, and that all other claims were nonsensical. Proofs should be brought by fantasy tellers and not by their listeners. That is the way science should work.

SS of the Ahnenerbe with their Tibetan hosts having a traditional meal

History recounts that Ernst Schäfer led this expedition with many difficulties due to his passage through British India just before the coming war. Despite these challenges, he and his team remained focused on geology, ethnology, botany, and zoology. They brought back to Germany many pictures, film rushes, samples of plants and animals, measurements, and precious gifts from their Tibetan hosts, like a complete edition of the Tibetan sacred text, the Kangyur, in 108 volumes, as well as other ancient texts, one of which was an alleged document regarding the Aryan race. It has also been said that the Schäfer team brought back a statue called the "Iron Man" made of meteoritic metal, likely as old as 1,000 years, dating from the pre-Buddhist Bon religion.

Although the expedition managed to navigate political tensions and logistical obstacles, it was conducted under the auspices of the Nazi SS and was influenced by ideological motivations. The artifacts they brought back were used primarily for propaganda purposes rather than for genuine academic interest in Tibetan culture.

Poland (1939): Wolfram Sievers convinced Himmler to loot certain museum pieces, like the famous Veit Stoss altarpiece in Cracow, but in many cases, Goering's men were quicker. The Ahnenerbe was mainly left with scientific devices and historical artifacts bearing little commercial value.

Crimea (1943): Himmler sent his men of the Ahnenerbe to pursue the Gothic relics that were supposed to exist in this region. These relics would have confirmed the presence of past Aryan tribes. Instead, they found just a few relics dating back to ancient Greek colonies established in the region and stone-age artifacts.

Ukraine (1943): Strange and mysterious botanic experiments were held in that region, perhaps in an effort to discover a resistant variety of wheat that would enable the Reich to feed its wartime population.

Cancelled expeditions

Once the war started, the Ahnenerbe had to cancel its planned expeditions because the British fleet was everywhere. Canceled expeditions included Tiwanaku (Bolivia), which was set out to prove that these remarkable gigantic pre-Columbian constructions could only have been built by ancient Aryan migrants; Behistun (Iran) to study the inscriptions about the Aryan origin of the Iranians, ordered by Shah Darius-I, which were found on top of a steep cliff; Canary Islands, where legends reported that the ancient inhabitants had blond hair, and where they had found mummies with these characteristics; and Iceland, to study ancient farming and architectural practices, as well as their folklore.

"Gateway of the Sun" at Tiwanaku

Human experiments

The most infamous attributes of the Ahnenerbe were their experiments on human beings, to test how far a human could resist in freezing waters, to try new medications, and so forth. Even a collection of Jewish skulls was ordered to facilitate racial measurements. These experiments made the whole Ahnenerbe a criminal organization, as sentenced by the Nuremberg Trials, which condemned Wolfram Sievers to death. It has been said that a Tibetan ritual chant was performed upon his dead body.

Much has been said about the Ahnenerbe, and the weirdest conspiracy theories have been propagated online or in cheap esoteric articles here and there. They are far from the truth, and they include tales about Nazi vampires, Übersoldaten, parallel universes only accessible to Nazi UFOs, etc. Though it is pure fiction, the most respectable work in that field is Steven Spielberg's Indiana Jones movie, which portrays how eager Nazi secret agents were to get a hold of the Holy Grail.

Chapter 15

The Castle of Wewelsburg

The Wewelsburg is a castle from the Renaissance era in North Rhine-Westphalia, Germany, close to Paderborn. The overall shape of the castle is triangular and dates back to the beginning of the 17th century, although some earlier strongholds had been built around that same place ever since the 9th century. It is worth mentioning that during the 17th century, many women were held prisoner in the dungeon under the accusation of witchcraft, and they were consequently tortured and then burned at the stake.

In 1934, Reichsführer Heinrich Himmler signed a lease of 100 years for one Reichsmark a year, with the intention of renovating the whole castle as an SS leadership school (*SS-Führerschule*). The works began first with volunteers of the *Reichsarbeitsdienst*, who were then replaced by forced labor from a nearby concentration camp. The bedrooms carried names of the Grail legend and King Arthur's adventures. The guests could also enjoy the use of a big dining room, an auditorium, a library, and even a photographic laboratory.

They trained in such fields as ideology, early history, archeology, mythology, and astronomy. Though it was already close to defeat, Himmler had thought about building a planetarium and recruiting an astronomer to teach the high-ranking cadre of the SS.

Wewelsburg Castle

The teachings later became more oriented towards a particular type of esotericism, made up of ancestral cults and practices (see Ahnenerbe), the study of the runes and racial theories, as well as the worshiping of nature. This whole education was to serve as a kind of new and mysterious pagan cult based on the legend of the Holy Grail and the Knights of the Round Table. New religious rituals were invented for this purpose, with the help of Karl Maria Wiligut, at least in the beginning, since his reputation and mental health were later questioned by many, even inside the SS.

Such rituals included SS marriages, most ancient pagan festivals, like the Yuletide, and the winter and summer solstices. Himmler, who admired Ignatius of Loyola's book *Spiritual Exercises*, allegedly practiced meditation with his higher-ranking generals (*Obergruppenführer*), although no hard evidence could ever be found except for the testimony of SS General Walter Schellenberg at the Nuremberg Trials. He described a curriculum consisting of "spiritual training and meditation exercises."

The Black Sun in the Gruppenführer hall of the Wewelsburg lies precisely above the swastika on the ceiling of the crypt underneath.

The most esoteric part of the castle was its North Tower, which was not destroyed even by the explosion at the end of the war and is, therefore, supposed to store "powerful magical energies." It was to be the very spiritual center of the Aryan world, extending then to the adjacent cities around the castle, which were to be drastically modified according to the grandiose blueprints found after the war.

The North Tower had a stone-lined room called the *Obergruppenführersaal* (SS Generals' Room), where the floor was inlaid with a Sun-Wheel symbol made of interlaced swastikas and sig runes, later to be called the Black Sun (see chapter on "The Black Sun"). The generals' coat of arms hung on the walls, and in the center of the room stood an oak Arthurian round table for the twelve senior SS generals. In the underlying crypt, or "Land of the Dead," were also twelve matching urns intended to receive the ashes of the generals when they died. The *Obergruppenführersaal* was used only once in 1941 before Operation Barbarossa, which was the invasion of Russia.

The crypt underneath (present day).

Himmler had asked in 1938 for a safe only the castle commandant and himself would know about. In the same mysterious, confidential way, all Death's Head rings (*Totenkopfring*) of dead SS men had to be returned to a shrine in the castle.

Due to the Allied advance, namely of the US Army, an SS commando was sent on March 31, 1945, to destroy the castle and hide all the Death's Head rings in a secret location in the neighboring mountains. These were never found, despite the zeal of generations of treasure hunters.

Chapter 16

The Witch Files

In 1935, Reichsführer Heinrich Himmler decided to build up a secret team of researchers in charge of gathering information about the persecution of witches and their trials throughout the ages. This research was named *Hexen-Sonderauftrag* or, more secretively, *H-Sonderauftrag* (Witch Special Operation). His SS gathered information not only in Germany but from other countries as well. They worked primarily undercover in German libraries and archives, pretending to look for their own genealogies. The 38,846 files were stocked in a *Hexenkartothek* (a witch file library). Each file stored information on why a given witch was imprisoned, the details of her trials, and the types of torture she was subjected to.

These files aimed to prove the wicked involvement of the Catholic Church and beyond in a Jewish conspiracy that was meant to destroy ancient Germanic creeds. The Christian faith had allegedly fought old pagan rituals in their most sacred places, like the famous Externsteine close to the Wewelsburg castle, where ancient rites were performed from the oldest times man can remember. Pagan priests and priestesses were, therefore, burned as sorcerers and witches. The cellars of Himmler's beloved Wewelsburg were used until the 17th century to imprison persons suspected of being "witches and werewolves."

Chronicle of Schilling of Lucerne (1513), illustrating the burning of a woman in Willisau (Switzerland) in 1447

Germany was indeed one of the European countries that murdered the most significant number of so-called witches, counting them by the tens of thousands. It is worth mentioning that Himmler was told by SS genealogists that among his ancestors, there was a witch who had been burned at the stake. This personal connection may have intensified Himmler's obsession with the subject and fueled his determination to expose what he perceived as a longstanding conspiracy against the Germanic people. The Brothers Grimm would also contribute to having the legend about the persecution of witches live on in their tales, further embedding the idea of witch hunts in German cultural consciousness.

Himmler believed that uncovering the truth about witch persecutions would help reveal a broader narrative of suppression that extended beyond religion and into the domain of cultural and racial identity. He saw the witch trials as a tool used by the Christian-Jewish conspiracy to erase Germanic heritage and enforce foreign values upon the German people. To Himmler, the witches represented the guardians of ancient wisdom and spiritual power that had been lost due to centuries of persecution. This belief led him to seek out remnants of this lost knowledge, which he believed could help restore the German people to their former greatness.

The *Hexenkartothek* was not merely a collection of historical records; it was part of a larger project to construct an ideological foundation for the Nazi regime. Himmler envisioned that the information gathered could be used to prove that the Aryan race had been systematically targeted and oppressed by external forces, which justified the regime's own brutal actions against those they deemed enemies. This approach aligned with Himmler's fascination with the occult and his belief that hidden, mystical forces played a significant role in shaping history.

Researches in the field of witch persecution were carried on until 1944, despite the ongoing war and the closing in of Allied forces from the West as well as from the East. The last order related to this occult quest, given by Himmler in 1944 to his staff, was to try to prove that Von Stauffenberg, the main perpetrator of the bomb plot against Hitler, had among his ancestors witch persecutors. This bizarre attempt to link the anti-Hitler conspirator to witch persecution showed just how deeply ingrained Himmler's beliefs were, even in the face of Germany's imminent defeat.

Interestingly, there were rumors that Himmler believed certain sites in Europe, particularly those associated with witch trials and executions, held residual occult power that could be harnessed. He allegedly ordered SS units to visit these locations and conduct rituals aimed at harnessing this power, though no concrete evidence of such practices has been found. This blend of myth, legend, and pseudo-history became an integral part of the Nazi mystique, reinforcing the idea that their struggle was not just political but also spiritual in nature.

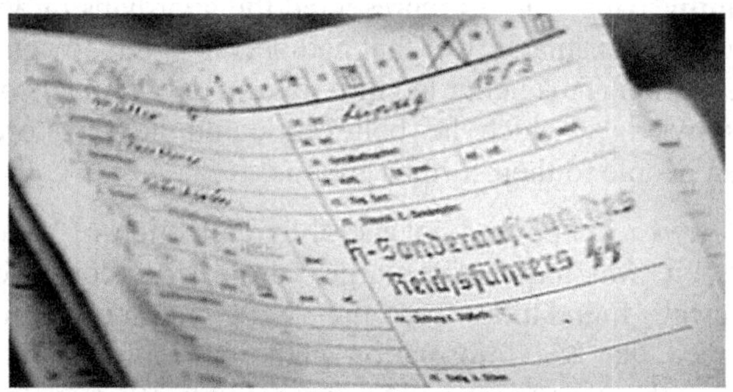

Files from the Witch Special Operation

None of the planned publications and books on the subject went through. What is left over from this incredible occultist search in the middle of the 20th century are the files of the Hexenkartothek: the originals are nowadays in Poznań (Poland), and a copy can be found on microfilms at the Bundesarchiv in Berlin. They are not of much interest to modern scholars since they were not collected according to the best scientific methods. However, they serve as a reminder of the strange and often irrational pursuits of the Nazi leadership, which mixed pseudoscience, occultism, and political ideology in an attempt to construct a mythic narrative that would justify their actions.

This case is real and has deep roots in the occult, but one must not deduce that Himmler wanted to cast spells on the Allies. His goal was only to prove a Christian-Jewish conspiracy against the ancient Aryans. Nevertheless, the sheer scope of the project and the resources dedicated to it highlight the extent to which the Nazi leadership was willing to delve into esoteric and mystical realms in their quest for legitimacy. This obsession with the occult also fueled conspiracy theories that have persisted to this day, with some claiming that the Nazis uncovered powerful occult secrets that were hidden away after the war. These claims, while lacking evidence, continue to captivate those interested in the mysterious and unexplainable aspects of history.

An alleged SS file about a Devil's Pact from 1653

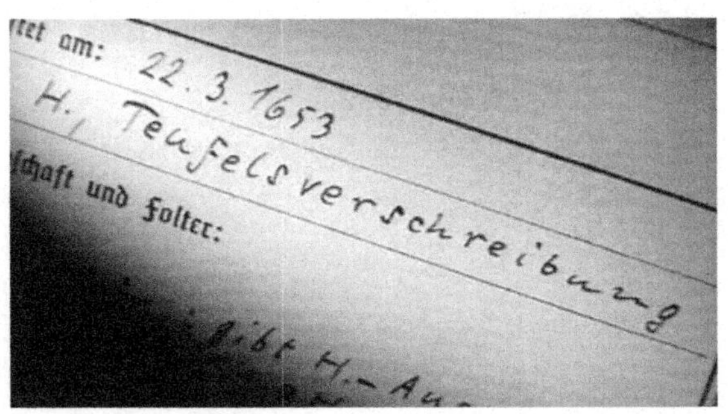

The Witch Files remain a fascinating example of how ideology can drive a regime to pursue fantastical and unscientific inquiries, blending historical fact, legend, and conspiracy theory into a narrative that served their political ends. The legacy of the *Hexenkartothek* is not in the value of its content but in what it reveals about the inner workings of the Nazi regime and their determination to construct a mythology that would support their claims of racial supremacy and justify their brutal actions. To this day, the Witch Files serve as a chilling reminder of how easily history can be twisted to serve nefarious purposes when driven by ideology rather than truth.

Chapter 17

Hitler and Magic

Much has been written in the field of pseudo-esotericism, and a makeshift evil genealogy of Hitler was made up in the later part of the 20th century, namely: he was Satan's medium, he sold his soul to the devil, he negotiated with Unknown Superiors from Shamballah, with extraterrestrials from Aldebaran, etc. Most of these claims were Allied propaganda aimed at discrediting him. Some even said that he was involved in abnormal sexual practices, BDSM, and the like. The truth is always stranger than fiction, though. This is the case with a book from Hitler's private library.

In the spring of 1945, the 101-St. Airborne Division found Hitler's library packed in crates and hidden in a salt mine near Berchtesgaden, where he had his Berghof Alpine chalet. Only 3,000 books out of the estimated more than 16,000 that he was supposed to own were found in different locations. These books were later sent to the United States Library of Congress in the early '50s. The discovery of these books, especially those dealing with occult and esoteric topics, fueled many conspiracy theories about Hitler's supposed dabbling in mysticism and supernatural powers.

The most serious authors, like Nicholas Goodrick-Clark, now dismiss the idea that Hitler was seriously interested or involved in occultism. There are nonetheless occult and esoteric books in Hitler's library from such authors as Adamant Rohm, a "magnetopathic doctor"; Carl Ludwig Schleich, a Berlin physician using local anesthesia; and Joseph Anton Schneiderfranken, aka Bô Yin Râ, who wrote books on reincarnation. The strangest and most marked book, though, is, undoubtedly, the one called *Magic: History, Theory, and Practice* (1923) by Ernst Schertel.

Ernst Schertel, an early advocate in the '20s of the German nudist movement, tackled themes linked with magic, demons, eroticism, sadomasochism, and flagellation. Schertel's work focused on exploring taboo subjects and the darker sides of human nature. He viewed magic as a means to reveal hidden potential and access primal forces. His book discussed the connections between magic and the subconscious mind, emphasizing the idea that those who were willing to explore forbidden knowledge could gain great power over themselves and others.

He dedicated a copy of his book to Adolf Hitler and sent it to him in 1923. This fact was made known to the public only in 2003 in an article published in *The Atlantic Monthly* by Timothy Ryback, the author of *Hitler's Private Library: The Books That Shaped His Life*. Among the passages Hitler marked, one can find the following: "False images are necessary for the recognition of truth"; "He who does not have the demonic seed within himself will never give birth to a magical world"; and "Satan is the beginning, Seraph is the end". These annotations suggest that Hitler was at least intrigued by the ideas presented by Schertel, particularly those concerning the nature of power, deception, and the manipulation of reality.

The presence of such a book in Hitler's library has led many to speculate about his true beliefs and motivations. Some argue that Hitler's fascination with power and manipulation could have drawn him to the esoteric concepts presented in Schertel's work, even if he ultimately dismissed much of it as impractical. It is also worth noting that Hitler was known to be an avid reader, and his interests spanned a wide range of topics, from history and politics to art and philosophy. The fact that he read a book on magic does not necessarily mean that he believed in or practiced magic, but it does indicate an openness to exploring different ideas, no matter how controversial or unconventional.

As a "reward," Dr. Ernst Schertel was sent to a concentration camp and stripped of his PhD during the time that the war lasted. This harsh treatment reflects the unpredictable and often contradictory nature of the Nazi regime, which simultaneously promoted certain occult ideas while brutally suppressing individuals who espoused them.

The idea that Hitler was deeply involved in the occult has been further popularized by various books, documentaries, and movies. One notable example is the previously mentioned book The Morning of the Magicians by Louis Pauwels and Jacques Bergier, which presents the notion that the Nazi leadership, including Hitler, was heavily influenced by esoteric and mystical beliefs. This book, along with others in the genre, helped to create a mythos around Hitler as a figure who was not only a political leader but also a dark magician or even a pawn of supernatural forces. Such claims have been largely discredited by historians, who point out that Hitler's real focus was always on political power and the implementation of his ideological vision for Germany.

Another theory suggests that Hitler's early exposure to the racist occult magazine *Ostara*, published by Jörg Lanz von Liebenfels, may have influenced his thinking. *Ostara* promoted a blend of Aryan mysticism, racial purity, and occultism, and it is believed that Hitler read these magazines while living in Vienna. This connection has led some to argue that Hitler's later actions were influenced by occult ideas about racial superiority and the destiny of the Aryan race. However, there is little concrete evidence to support the idea that Hitler's interest in *Ostara* extended beyond a brief fascination during his formative years.

Later in his life and even in *Mein Kampf*, Hitler made fun of astrologers, mediums, seers, and all "the occult rubbish" Himmler was so much involved in. Heinrich Himmler, on the other hand, was deeply fascinated by the occult and actively promoted the study of esoteric subjects within the SS, including astrology, rune magic, and ancient Germanic paganism. Himmler believed that such knowledge could be used to strengthen the Nazi regime and establish a spiritual connection with Germany's ancient past. Hitler, however, saw these pursuits as distractions and often ridiculed Himmler's obsession with the mystical.

The contrast between Hitler's pragmatic approach to power and Himmler's occult fascination highlights the complex relationship between the Nazi leadership and the esoteric. While Himmler and others within the SS were enthusiastic about using occult symbols and rituals to legitimize their authority, Hitler remained focused on the practical aspects of gaining and maintaining control. This does not mean that Hitler was entirely dismissive of the power of myth and symbolism—he was well aware of their importance in shaping public perception and used them effectively in his propaganda—but he did not share Himmler's belief in the literal power of the occult.

Chapter 18

Wotan and the Aryan Archetype

Swiss psychoanalyst Carl Gustav Jung had a profound interest in archetypical explanations of Nazism, viewing them as closely related to a semi-religious paradigm. Jung's fascination with mythology and the collective unconscious made him uniquely suited to analyze the phenomenon of Nazism. He believed that the rise of Hitler and the fervor of the Nazi movement were deeply connected to the archetypes that lay dormant in the German psyche, particularly the figure of Wotan, the ancient Norse god associated with chaos, war, and inspiration.

Jung maintained a dense correspondence for some time with Miguel Serrano, the Chilean Nazi diplomat, about psychology and more esoteric topics related to Jung's archetype theory. Serrano, who was an advocate of esoteric Hitlerism, believed in the existence of a hidden, mystical truth that could explain the rise of Nazism. Jung's discussions with Serrano often revolved around the concept of archetypes as powerful forces that could shape both individual and collective behavior. These archetypes, according to Jung, were part of the collective unconscious—a shared reservoir of symbols, myths, and memories that influence human actions on a deep, often unconscious level.

In his essay, first published in 1936 in Zurich as *Wotan* in the *Neue Schweizer Rundschau*, when writing about Nazism in Germany, Jung suggests, "Perhaps we may sum up this general phenomenon as Ergriffenheit – a state of being seized or possessed. The term postulates an Ergriffener (one who is seized) and an Ergreifer (one who seizes). Wotan is an Ergreifer of men, and unless one wishes to deify Hitler – which did indeed actually happen – he is really the only explanation." Jung's invocation of Wotan as the archetypal force behind Hitler's rise was a striking attempt to explain the irrational and almost mystical power that Hitler seemed to wield over the German people. Wotan, also known as Odin in Norse mythology, was a god of frenzy, inspiration, and transformation, traits that Jung saw reflected in the fervor of the Nazi movement.

Jung believed that the figure of Wotan had been reawakened in the German collective unconscious, leading to a resurgence of primal, instinctual energies that manifested in the form of Nazism. This idea of being "seized" by an archetypal force was central to Jung's understanding of the Nazi phenomenon. He argued that Hitler was not merely a political leader but a vessel for the archetypal energies of Wotan, which had taken hold of the German people. This view of Hitler as an archetype, rather than an individual, helped Jung make sense of the almost hypnotic effect that Hitler had on his followers.

Furthermore, in the book *Black Sun*, Nicholas Goodrick-Clarke writes how Carl Jung showed "Hitler as possessed by the archetype of the collective Aryan unconscious, and could not help obeying the commands of an inner voice." Hitler often referred to his "inner voice" and the Providence that helped him during many difficult moments of his life. This inner voice, Jung suggested, was the manifestation of the collective unconscious, a deeper force that guided Hitler's actions and decisions. To Jung, Hitler's sense of destiny and his belief in his own infallibility were signs that he was operating under the influence of an archetypal power that transcended his individual personality.

Wotan, aka Odin, the Norse God

Wotan, aka Odin, the Norse God, was a complex figure who embodied both the creative and destructive aspects of human nature. Jung saw these dual aspects reflected in Hitler's rise to power—on the one hand, Hitler was able to inspire and unite the German people, while on the other hand, he unleashed a wave of destruction and chaos that ultimately led to the downfall of Germany. Jung's analysis of Hitler as an archetype was not an attempt to excuse his actions but rather to understand the deeper psychological forces at play.

Carl Jung thought of Hitler as an archetype, often manifesting itself to the complete exclusion of his own personality. "There is no question but that Hitler belongs in the category of the truly mystic medicine man. As somebody commented about him at the last Nürnberg party congress, since the time of Mohammed nothing like it has been seen in this world. His body does not suggest strength. The outstanding characteristic of his physiognomy is its dreamy look. I was especially struck by that when I saw pictures taken of him in the Czechoslovakian crisis; there was in his eyes the look of a seer. This markedly mystic characteristic of Hitler's is what makes him do things which seem to us illogical, inexplicable, and unreasonable. ... So you see, Hitler is a medicine man, a spiritual vessel, a demi-deity or, even better, a myth."

This brings us to all the underground theories about Hitler as a medium of Higher Powers, as they were brought up by less serious authors. These theories suggest that Hitler was not acting on his own volition but was instead a conduit for higher, possibly supernatural forces. While Jung himself did not endorse these theories, his portrayal of Hitler as a mythic figure lent itself to such interpretations.

Jung's writings on Wotan and Hitler have been interpreted in many ways, some more speculative than others. The idea that Hitler was a medium for higher powers has been taken up by various fringe authors and conspiracy theorists, who argue that the Nazi regime was influenced by occult forces. These theories often draw on Jung's description of Hitler as being "possessed" by an archetype, suggesting that he was in contact with entities or energies beyond the material world. While these claims lack credible evidence, they reflect the enduring fascination with the idea of Hitler as more than just a political leader—as a figure shrouded in mystery and darkness.

The connection between Wotan and Hitler also highlights the role of mythology in shaping political ideologies. Jung believed that the power of myth could not be underestimated, as it had the ability to reach the deepest layers of the human psyche. The Nazi regime, under the influence of figures like Heinrich Himmler, actively sought to revive ancient Germanic myths and symbols as a way of legitimizing their rule and creating a sense of national identity. The use of symbols like the swastika and the emphasis on Aryan heritage were part of an attempt to connect the present with a mythic past, one that was imagined as pure, heroic, and untainted by modernity.

Jung's analysis of the Nazi movement as a manifestation of the Wotan archetype provides a unique perspective on the psychological underpinnings of totalitarianism. It suggests that the rise of such movements is not merely a result of political or economic factors but is also driven by deeper, unconscious forces that can seize hold of entire populations. The figure of Wotan, with his unpredictable and chaotic nature, served as a fitting symbol for the energies that had been unleashed in Germany during the 1930s and 1940s. These energies, once awakened, could not be easily controlled, leading to the catastrophic events of World War II.

Rather than providing a definitive conclusion, Jung's exploration of Wotan and Hitler invites us to consider the profound impact of mythology and the unconscious on human history. The archetype of Wotan, with its blend of creativity and destruction, serves as a reminder of the potential for both greatness and horror that lies within the human psyche—an open door to understanding how myths and collective archetypes continue to influence modern societies and political movements.

Part Three

Shadows of the Reich

Chapter 19

The Morning of the Magicians

The Morning of the Magicians is a book written in 1960 by Pauwels and Bergier in France. It was a best-seller and subsequently translated into many languages. The book's content consisted mainly of thrilling stories, which were, as such, mostly unsubstantiated on a historical and scientific level.

They tackled many subjects like ancient astronauts, spiritism, and out-of-place artifacts, and they dedicated a whole section to Nazi esotericism. The way they presented this "breach in the fabric of history" was not entirely new; they followed in the footsteps of earlier authors from the early 1930s, mainly French writers, who were among the first to associate Hitler with dark forces or even portray him as the devil incarnate.

Pauwels and Bergier mixed entirely unknown but genuine facts about the Nazi era with pure fantasies, many of which were the product of their own imagination. They mentioned the now well-known Hörbiger's theories about the Ice World, its falling moons, and the subsequent sinking of Atlantis. The authors also included the Hollow Earth Theory, the Thule Society, and the inevitable Vril Society. In doing so, they crafted a narrative that blended authentic historical elements with mystical and occult speculation, creating an intriguing but often misleading portrayal of the Third Reich.

We took the trouble to quote some pertinent experts' opinions. However, Pauwels and Bergier fabricated an entirely different life for Professor Haushofer, claiming he was a member of the secret society of the Green Dragon in Japan and that he committed the Japanese hara-kiri ritual to end his life just after the war, supposedly fulfilling a promise to his Asian initiators. These claims were never substantiated by any credible historical evidence, further blurring the line between fact and fiction in their work.

Asian Volunteers from Turkestan in the German Army (France)

Our hallucinating authors mentioned the presence of "Tibetan" dead bodies, wearing German uniforms without any insignia, in the ruins of Berlin in 1945. There is, however, not a single piece of historical proof of this happening; at best, they could have been misled by the documented participation of foreign volunteers from Central Asia, who had been "liberated" by the

Nazis from the Stalinist regime. These Central Asian recruits, including volunteers from Turkestan, were often integrated into German units with minimal identification, which may have led to confusion and exaggerated claims of Tibetan forces.

Hermann Rauschning (1887 – 1982)

The book's most notable contribution was its role in popularizing various myths about the occult roots of Nazism. This is perhaps best exemplified in *The Morning of the Magicians*' reference to Hermann Rauschning's *Hitler Speaks*. In their retelling, Pauwels and Bergier did not hesitate to reiterate the now-famous, dramatic description of Hitler allegedly hearing voices, waking at night with convulsive shrieks, and pointing in terror at an empty corner of the room while shouting, "There, there, in the corner!" The vivid depiction of Hitler's supposed supernatural experiences fit neatly into their broader narrative of the occult influences on the Nazi regime.

According to most modern researchers, Rauschning's book was a fraud. Hänel, a Swiss scholar who studied the book in detail, notes that:

- Rauschning's claim to have met with Hitler "more than a hundred times" was a lie, as the two men met only four times, and never alone.

- Certain words he attributed to Hitler were inspired by many different sources, including the writings of Ernst Jünger, Nietzsche, and the French writer Guy de Maupassant in his short novel *Le Horla.*

- M. Emery Reves, the publisher of the original French edition of *Hitler Speaks*, claimed that he commissioned the book from Rauschning in 1939 for 125,000 francs in advance, and they agreed on the fabricated stories about Hitler to be written in that book.

Nowadays, no serious historian quotes Rauschning's book anymore. This is particularly the case for Hitler's most prominent academic biographer, Ian Kershaw, who stated, "I have on no single occasion cited Hermann Rauschning's *Hitler Speaks*, a work now regarded to have so little authenticity that it is best to disregard it altogether." Despite this, Pauwels and Bergier's work continued to rely on such contested sources, further adding to the aura of mystery surrounding the Nazi era.

The Morning of the Magicians remains an influential but controversial work, blurring the lines between myth and reality in its treatment of the Nazi era and other esoteric themes. Its legacy can be seen in the numerous books, films, and documentaries that have since sought to explore the supposed occult underpinnings of Hitler's regime. Although many of the book's claims have been debunked, the fascination with these "hidden histories" endures, inviting us to consider why such myths persist and what they reveal about our collective need for extraordinary explanations of historical events.

Chapter 20

Hitler's Death

The death of Adolf Hitler is one of the most enduring sources of modern myth, conspiracy, and fascination. The circumstances surrounding his demise in the final days of World War II, combined with the chaos of Berlin's fall, have provided fertile ground for endless speculation. The key ingredient for these myths is the mystery that surrounded Hitler's disappearance at the time. When the Russians finally reached Hitler's bunker in Berlin on May 2, 1945, it was empty. The person who had been identified as the Devil on Earth had vanished at the very last moment, giving rise to numerous survival theories. The fact that there were no indisputable eyewitnesses to his death added fuel to the fire, leading many to believe that Hitler had managed to escape. Even powerful organizations like the FBI and the KGB were drawn into the mystery, investigating rumors, sightings, and supposed clues for many years after the war ended.

The FBI finally closed the case of Hitler's death in 1956 after years of investigation that spanned several continents. They interviewed numerous individuals in the United States and

South America, often chasing after bizarre leads, but they eventually concluded that Hitler had died in the bunker. In contrast, the KGB never entirely gave up its suspicions, mainly due to Stalin's own paranoia. Stalin refused to publicly acknowledge that Hitler had committed suicide in Berlin, thus perpetuating the uncertainty around his fate. He had a vested interest in keeping the myth alive, possibly as a means of maintaining pressure on the Western Allies and sowing fear about a potential Nazi resurgence.

EXTRA THE STARS AND STRIPES EXTRA

HITLER DEAD

Churchill Hints Peace Is at Hand

Newspaper headline

Stalin was so consumed by paranoia that he ordered his secret police, the NKVD (which was a precursor to the KGB), to leave no stone unturned in unraveling Hitler's private life. He considered Hitler to be his greatest adversary, and the idea that he might have slipped through the Soviet net was an intolerable thought. As a result, the NKVD compiled an in-depth dossier on Hitler's final days, which was intended for Stalin's eyes only. This dossier, later discovered by German researchers in the archives of Moscow, was eventually published in 2005 as *The Hitler Book: The Secret Dossier Prepared for Stalin from the Interrogations of Hitler's Personal Aides*, compiled by Henrik Eberle. The dossier provides an intimate glimpse into the lives of Hitler's close circle and offers additional details about his death that were previously unavailable to the public.

Despite this, the rumors of Hitler's escape persisted. Several books have been published claiming that Hitler fled to South America, where he lived to a very old age. Some claimed he lived well into his 90s, while other versions were even more outrageous, asserting that he lived beyond 110 years. One of the most well-known proponents of this theory is Jerome R. Corsi, a conspiracy theorist who argued in his book *Hunting Hitler* that Hitler escaped with the help of the CIA. According to Corsi, the CIA facilitated Hitler's flight to Argentina in exchange for access to valuable German technology. It is an improbable scenario, but it has captured the imagination of many readers, adding another layer of mystery to the story of Hitler's death.

Another intriguing twist comes from Brazilian writer Simoni Renee Guerreiro Dias, who proposed an even stranger story. In her book *Hitler in Brazil – His Life and His Death*, she argued that Hitler escaped to Brazil rather than Argentina, where he lived with a Black lover until the age of 95. Guerreiro Dias presented a blurry photograph, allegedly taken in the 1970s, depicting Hitler with his mistress, supposedly as a way of avoiding detection through his anti-racist behavior. The photo, however, has not been substantiated and remains highly controversial, adding to the many bizarre accounts of Hitler's supposed post-war survival.

The fate of Hitler's remains has also been a point of much speculation, partly due to the secrecy surrounding Soviet actions in the aftermath of Berlin's fall. The Soviet military intelligence unit SMERSH (whose name translates as "Death to Spies") found the remains of Hitler, Eva Braun, and two dogs in a shell crater near the bunker on May 2, 1945. By May 11, the SMERSH team had confirmed the identity of the remains through the testimony of Hitler's dentist's assistant, whom they had located after days of searching in the ruins of Berlin. This confirmation was based primarily on dental records, which were crucial in positively identifying Hitler.

Rear entrance to the Führerbunker (1947)

Even after confirming the identity of the remains, the Soviets took great pains to ensure that Hitler's body could not be used as a rallying point for neo-Nazi elements. In 1946, the remains of Hitler and Braun were secretly transported by SMERSH to a Soviet barracks in Magdeburg, East Germany, where they were buried in crates. There they remained, buried in secrecy, until 1970. As the Soviet Union prepared to hand over its Magdeburg facilities to East Germany, the KGB director at the time, Yuri Andropov, wrote a letter to the Soviet Premier Leonid Brezhnev requesting permission to destroy the remains. Andropov's reasoning was that the remains, if discovered, could become a shrine for neo-Nazi sympathizers, thereby threatening stability in the Eastern Bloc.

On April 4, 1970, a secret KGB team was dispatched to Magdeburg to carry out Andropov's request. Guided by detailed maps and burial charts, they exhumed five wooden boxes containing the remains of 10 or 11 bodies, which possibly included members of the Goebbels family. The remains were in an advanced state of decay, making identification difficult. These remains were then burned once again, crushed into ashes, and scattered into the Biederitz River, a tributary of the Elbe, near Schönebeck, a town not far from Magdeburg. This final act was intended to ensure that there would be no physical trace of Hitler left for anyone to find.

Wooden box where Hitler's alleged remains were found.

Hitler was determined to avoid falling into the hands of the advancing Soviets alive, knowing full well that he would be subjected to public humiliation similar to what had happened to Mussolini, whose body had been strung up in Milan for public display after his execution. By disappearing in the bunker, Hitler believed he was orchestrating a grand finale—a final act of defiance that ensured that his body could not be desecrated or exploited. This deliberate vanishing act fed into the mythology that he had somehow managed to escape, leaving behind just enough ambiguity to ensure that the legend of his supposed survival would endure for decades.

The continuing fascination with Hitler's death—the conflicting accounts, the conspiracy theories, and the secrecy—highlights the powerful allure of unresolved mysteries. Whether it was Stalin's paranoia, the conflicting testimonies of witnesses, or the Soviets' secretive handling of his remains, each of these factors contributed to a narrative that has refused to be completely laid to rest. The story of Hitler's death remains shrouded in the very elements that make for compelling historical fiction: suspense, secrecy, and the possibility—however slim—that the truth may be different from the accepted version. This enduring interest also reveals our collective fascination with the idea that evil might not be fully vanquished, that somewhere in the shadows, remnants of the past might still lurk, waiting to resurface.

Chapter 21

The Mystic Treasure of the SS

According to Saint-Loup, a French author of many books about the history of the French volunteers of the Waffen-SS Division Charlemagne who fought Bolshevism in the Soviet Union, the SS treasure is a great secret. Saint-Loup is a pen name for Marc Augier, a French collaborator, great sportsman, and journalist who was deeply involved in Nazi ideology and has remained a controversial figure in France. His writings cast a romanticized glow over the Waffen-SS, presenting them as defenders of Europe rather than the perpetrators of some of the worst atrocities of the war.

In many of his books, Saint-Loup presents the SS as a noble order, much like a modern version of the Teutonic Knights. He gives them an aura of heroism and positions them as the self-declared guardians of the Aryan race in a "decadent" post-war world. What makes them especially attractive in his narrative is the idea that they possess the great secret of the Aryan race, the one and only secret capable of saving the white race from vanishing from the surface of the earth.

According to Saint-Loup, this great secret was carved on stone tablets by the Cathars in the 13th century in France, at the time of the fall of the Montségur castle, the last bastion of the Cathar resistance against the Crusaders. The Cathars were a Christian Gnostic sect known for their heretical views, and they are surrounded by legends of mystical knowledge and hidden treasures. These tablets are depicted as an Aryan equivalent to the stone tablets on which Moses wrote the Ten Commandments—except that, in Saint-Loup's version, the Aryans do not fully understand the origins or significance of their tablets and have lost track of their true meaning over the centuries.

Saint-Loup in 1942 in Smolensk in German uniform

Otto Rahn, a scholar fascinated by Cathar mythology and the Grail legends, allegedly discovered these tablets. Rahn was a specialist in Roman languages and literature and an SS officer who reported directly to the infamous Ahnenerbe, the SS organization tasked with uncovering "evidence" of Aryan superiority through historical, archaeological, and anthropological research. Rahn's obsession with the occult led him on numerous expeditions to uncover sacred artifacts that would legitimize Nazi ideology and elevate the SS to a near-religious status. According to the legend popularized by Saint-Loup, Rahn brought the tablets back to Germany but met a mysterious and tragic end soon afterward. He was found frozen to death in the Bavarian Alps in 1939—though he was an excellent mountain climber, leading some to speculate whether his death was truly an accident or an assassination ordered to ensure the secrecy of his discoveries.

The Zillertal around 1898

The mystery thickened as World War II came to a close. With the Allies closing in on the Alpine Fortress, Saint-Loup claims that on May 2, 1945, a special SS unit made only of officers from various European nationalities gathered in Tyrol, Austria, at the crossroads of Innsbruck-Salzburg and Gmünd-Zell am

Ziller. The unit was composed of men from across Nazi-occupied Europe, including French, Belgian, Scandinavian, and even some British and American volunteers who had joined the Waffen-SS. They were not ordinary soldiers but carefully selected individuals who had pledged their lives to protect the great secret.

The day before, three high-ranking SS officers—comprising a Frenchman, a Norwegian, and an American—were reportedly taken on a covert mission, possibly to Tibet, by a long-range aircraft that landed on the Munich-Salzburg highway. This bizarre claim ties into another thread of Nazi mythology, which suggests that the Third Reich had secret alliances with mystical Tibetan lamas or other unknown Asian powers that supposedly held esoteric wisdom and knowledge about the Aryan race.

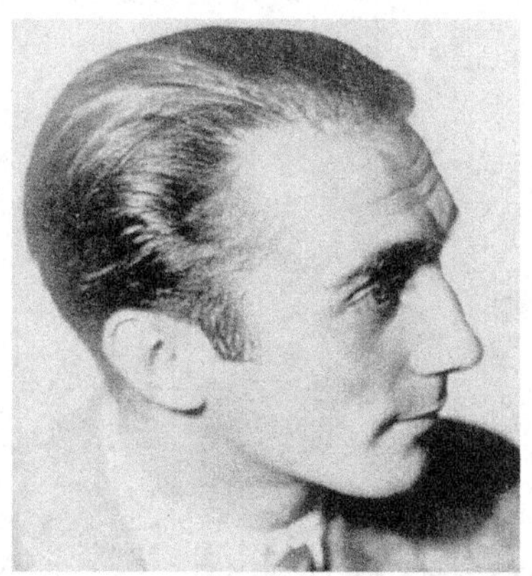

Otto Rahn

The rest of the SS unit was stationed in the Tyrolean Alps, awaiting something of immense importance. It was their sworn duty to hold off the advancing Allied forces for as long as possible. Eventually, a convoy coming from Berchtesgaden—Hitler's famous Alpine retreat—transferred to the SS unit a crate made of lead. This mysterious crate, according to Saint-Loup, contained the stone tablets originally found by Otto

Rahn. Their mission was to take the crate to the top of the Zillertal glacier and bury it there, hoping that the glacier's slow movement would eventually carry it down to the valley floor sometime between 1990 and 1995, when it could be rediscovered by future generations.

The secrecy surrounding this mission was intense. The officers involved were rumored to have taken oaths that included committing suicide rather than allowing the crate's contents to be discovered by outsiders. The secret inside the lead crate was so vital that it had to be read by all Aryans, or else, as they believed, the entire white world would be doomed to chaos and destruction.

According to Saint-Loup, the tablets bore a message that the Aryan race must adhere to the "holy rule" of not mixing their blood with "inferior races" if they were to avoid extinction. This gnostic and Manichaean belief portrayed all non-whites—and especially all Jews—as inherently evil, and claimed that the Holy Grail was a metaphor for pure Aryan blood. This notion of racial purity was central to Nazi ideology, as reflected in their brutal eugenics program, their obsession with genealogy, and their exterminationist policies.

Adding to the layers of myth, conspiracy theorists later claimed that the tablets also held secrets of an ancient and advanced technology, potentially linked to the lost civilization of Atlantis. The Nazis, and especially Heinrich Himmler, believed that Atlantis was the ancestral homeland of the Aryans, a technologically advanced civilization that was destroyed in a great cataclysm. Some believe that the tablets contained knowledge from Atlantis—scientific secrets that could give the Aryan race dominance over the rest of the world.

Interestingly, Saint-Loup's narrative draws heavily on elements of Arthurian legend, with the Aryan tablets serving as a Nazi equivalent to the Holy Grail—a mystical object with the power to save or redeem. The SS officers on their final mission are portrayed as modern-day Grail knights, tasked with preserving the sacred knowledge for future generations. This romanticized view of the SS contributed significantly to the post-war allure of Nazi mysticism, particularly among those who wished to see the SS as noble warriors rather than war criminals.

There are also suggestions that the treasure hunt for the Aryan tablets was part of a broader Nazi project to find esoteric artifacts that would confirm their beliefs in Aryan superiority. Himmler himself believed that by finding these ancient artifacts and proving the historical importance of the Aryans, he could establish the legitimacy of the Nazi regime not just politically, but spiritually as well.

The story of the mystic treasure of the SS has persisted in neo-Nazi circles and among enthusiasts of the occult. The symbolism of the hidden tablets, buried in ice and waiting to be discovered, serves as a powerful metaphor for the belief that the "true" history of the Aryan race has been suppressed by mainstream society and will one day be revealed to vindicate Nazi ideology. For some, it represents a kind of hope—a belief that the ideals of the Third Reich were not entirely defeated but merely went underground, waiting for the right moment to resurface.

Chapter 22

Fantasy Wonder Weapons

The German Wonder Weapons were so ahead of their time that they seemed to come from the future. However, this is not a good reason to make up stories about their origin that are not only ridiculous in their conception but also totally fraudulent in nature.

Die Glocke

One of the weirdest and most fraudulent post-war fictions is certainly *Die Glocke* (in German, The Bell). Igor Witkowski, a Polish journalist, claimed in 2000 that he had access to secret SS files talking about the purported existence of *Die Glocke* in his book called the *Prawda O Wunderwaffe* (The Truth About the Wonder Weapons).

As usual with this kind of fantasy, Witkowski cannot name the Polish intelligence source that gave him this information "for obvious security reasons." This did not prevent British author Nick Cook from seriously using this fantasy material as historical truth in his book *The Hunt for Zero Point* and reaching for the usual eager-to-believe-anything audience of science-fiction amateurs.

This prompted Joseph P. Farrell, author of *The SS Brotherhood of the Bell: Nasa's Nazis, JFK, and Majic-12*, to use Witkowski's claims to reignite the overall lowering interest that readers were beginning to show in Nazi occultist hodgepodge. It's funny how all these English-language writers who came forth as “we have the secret information" had to wait for years after an unknown Polish journalist first made revelations about *Die Glocke*. None of these authors bother to share their sources nor refrain from frantic science-fiction fabrications.

The Henge in Poland

Die Glocke was allegedly invented by Nazi scientists, helped by Jewish prisoners, as a way to travel through time and space using anti-gravitational science.

It was built in the underground facilities of Der Riese, which genuinely existed, as we already saw above. It was "made out of a hard, heavy metal approximately 9 feet wide and 12 to 15 feet high, with a shape similar to that of a large bell." Two counter-rotating cylinders filled with a mercury-like substance achieved the anti-gravitational effect.

Cooling Tower in Siechnice, Poland. Does it ring a bell?

Witkowski claims that the metal-and-concrete ruins in Poland called "The Henge," close to the Wenceslas mines, would have served as a test rig for the experiments related to *Die Glocke*. Such structures can be found in nearby places in the same Polish region but are nothing more than the cooling towers of power plants.

The funny part is that none of these writers agree on how the story ends. Farrell makes the Nazis kill no less than 60 scientists that contributed to the project to maintain its secrecy.

Witkowski claims that *Die Glocke* ended up somewhere in South America. Cook, for his part, states that it was taken over by the Americans, probably as part of Operation Paperclip. There are even well-known and usually serious TV channels that dramatize these versions. They showed a *Glocke* chained to The Henge, trying to fly away during a Doctor Evil-like experiment with many stunning 3D special effects.

Once more, of course, the evil SS General Hans Kammler is part of the plot. According to the different versions of the story, he either negotiated with the Americans or literally disappeared from the face of the Earth, maybe even from our space-time reality!

Strahlkanone

This was at least one actual project meant to send a lethal light ray against the Allied forces, something that one might call a "laser gun" nowadays.

Alleged picture of a similar project: a Schallkanone ("Sound Gun")

Nothing is known precisely about this mysterious plan, except that a professor Ernst Schiebold from Leipzig, once managed to get funds from the Nazi government to materialize this fantastic wonder weapon. More recently, his ex-secretary testified on German television about the reality of the project.

Still, she admitted that she was never allowed to get into the bunker where the actual experiments took place. Once that project was stopped, nobody heard of Professor Schiebold anymore.

This is not the typical case of a genuine "fantasy wonder weapon," but it lacks the thicker documentation required to distinguish facts from fiction. It is atypical enough to belong to the category of "intended wonder weapons" that did not succeed in turning the tide of the war against the Allies because they were still at the earlier stages of being either prototypes or blueprints.

Nazi UFOs

In Internet sci-fi underground lore and the thriving world of conspiracy theories, there circulate unsubstantiated claims that the Third Reich somehow managed to produce futuristic flying devices far ahead of the scientific capabilities of their times. These so-called Nazi UFOs have even German names to make them more credible: *Rundflugzeug, Feuerball, Diskus, Haunebu, Hauneburg-Geräte, V7, VRIL, Kugelblitz, Andromeda-Geräte, Flugkreisel, Kugelwaffen,* and *Reichsflugscheiben.* Many blueprints of these devices can be found on the Internet, all of them grossly concocted in German with "original Nazi fonts" and precise measurements to add a realistic touch.

These Nazi UFO fantasies stem mainly from 3 origins:

1– The allegedly wider scopes and achievements of the actual 1938-1939 German expedition to Antarctica in Neuschwabenland; Colin Summerhayes of the Scott Polar Institute scientifically debunked all claims that there ever were German bases in Antarctica (see chapter on Antarctica Expedition 1938-1939).

2– The significant advances that the Nazis possessed in rocketry and the purported findings of Dr. Viktor Schauberger in the field of breaking new means of propulsion (his famous "Repulsine" engine). Some scientists proved, however, that his Repulsine was no more than a water turbine on which he was working to cool aircraft engines at the Messerschmitt plants.

Original Repulsine device

Repulsine appears sometimes as a UFO.

3– The Allied sightings of so-called "Foo Fighters," allegedly German secret weapons designed to harass an aircraft through electromagnetic disruption. Though real, the German pilots saw the same phenomena and asked themselves what they could be and where they possibly came from.

Unfortunately for true amateurs of such mysterious stories, there are just unsubstantiated books and unscientific websites that address this subject. The eagerness of the writers to make money or, in the best cases, to prove their claim leads them more often than not to put together unrelated facts and draw hasty conclusions from similar events that either did or didn't take place at that same time or place. Their sources are anonymous "deep throats" for "obvious security reasons" or based on other such books and websites as serious as their own. They feed on one another, and people who dare criticize them are usually considered to be part of "government cover-up operations" at worst or very skeptical shrinks at best.

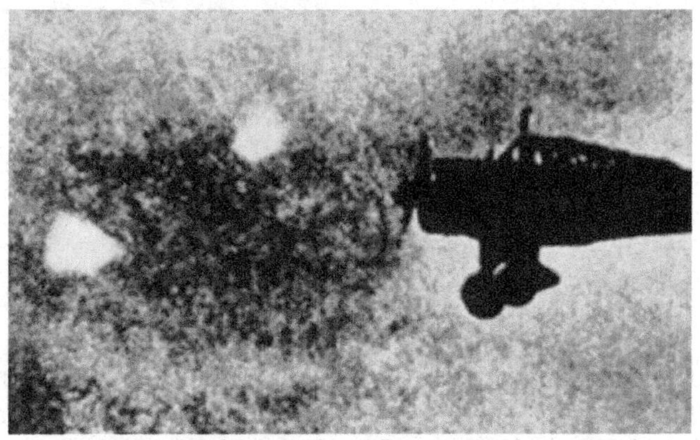

Rare picture of Foo Fighters flying around an aircraft

Some of the first reports on flying saucers, like Kenneth Arnold's in 1947, involved even the US military since their alleged shape was very similar to that of the Horten Brothers' Flying Wing. They eventually concluded that although the Germans were far ahead of their time in aeronautics, their plans were only blueprints or unreliable prototypes by the time the war ended.

A little bit later in the UFO wave, a Polish-American citizen named Adamski claimed to have made encounters of the third kind, like having made actual contact with ETs. These first extraterrestrials had this very odd feature of resembling the "perfect Aryans"; they were tall, blond, and blue-eyed, though pretending to come from Venus.

Adamski even took a picture of their spacecraft, but the only problem is that it was later proved to be a ... simple street lamp. This finding has not prevented this picture from being used, and reused on the Internet as a model for so-called Nazi UFOs, sometimes digitalized as a 3D model with the Luftwaffe cross on it.

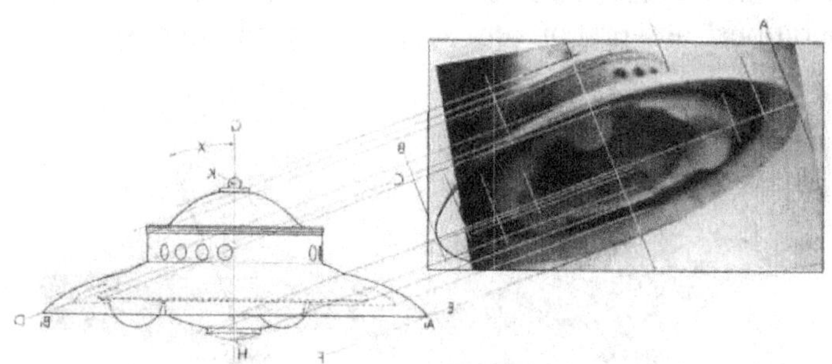

A "Nazi UFO" blueprint (left) and Adamski's street lamp (right).

The first links made between UFOs and Nazis are the work of the Italian professor Giuseppe Belluzzo, a scientist and former Minister of National Economy under the Mussolini regime. He claimed in 1950 that "types of flying discs were designed and studied in Germany and Italy as early as 1942."

There have also been subsequent claims that underground FIAT factories, mainly located in vast tunnels around the Lake of Garda in Italy, were used to produce Nazi UFOs. These stories were propagated by the Italian Renato Vesco, who claimed, among others, to have studied at a German Aeronautical Institute during the war but was later discredited because of discrepancies concerning his very young age at the time.

In 1950 the famous German magazine *Der Spiegel* tackled the subject of possible Nazi UFOs for the first time and reported the dubious stories of former engineer Rudolf Schriever and his round-flying device.

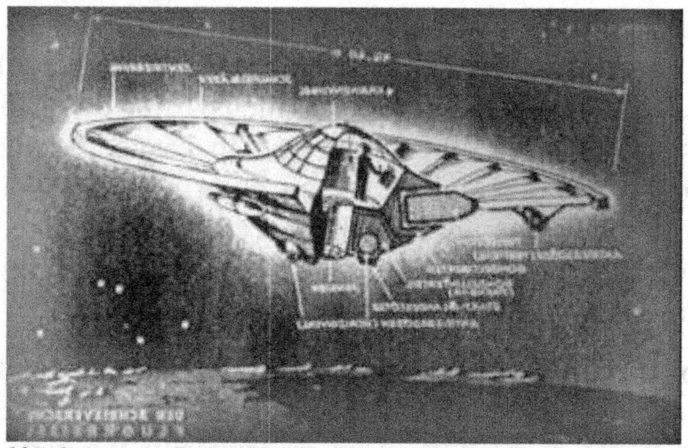

Rudolf Schriever's flying device as it appeared in Der Spiegel (1950)

Schriever did indeed show discrepancies in later versions of the same story, notably in 1952 during another interview.

Prototype of the Sack AS-6

True enough, some prototypes that never achieved mass production status, like the Sack AS-6, had a shape very close to those of the after-war UFO sightings.

The soar of Nazi UFOs is nevertheless historically attributed to writers like Jan van Helsing, Norbert-Jürgen Ratthofer, and

Vladimir Terziski, who developed the background stories and added to them detailed features to become the sophisticated myths of the '80s and '90s still known today. They mixed up the Thule and the Vril societies and invented the Vril girls (among whom we find the famous Maria Orsitsch), who established alleged contacts with aliens from the Albebaran star system, thanks to their long hair that acted as antennae. From these contacts and a crashed UFO found in the Black Forest in 1936, they would have reverse-engineered alien technology to produce all the flying machines you can see in the Antarctica sky today!

Some of these writers had even rightist political agendas and surfed on the Nazi occultist wave initiated by Pauwels and Bergier in the early '60s. This is primarily the case of the Vienna Circle with Wilhelm Landig at its head, as we already mentioned. On the other hand, a famous Holocaust denier by the name of Ernst Zündel almost admitted in an interview that he used the UFO madness to draw attention to his books and beliefs. He even tried to organize a trip to Antarctica for a $9,999 fee per seat to locate the polar entrance to the Hollow Earth, but the project did not go through. Finally, right-wing extremists like Miguel Serrano seem to believe in their own stories genuinely and have largely contributed to the Nazi sub-genre of UFO sightings and SS esotericism.

In popular culture, we find such harmless works as Robert Heinlein's book *Rocket Ship Galileo* (1947); it was a popular book for children that got special public attention for showing a Nazi base on the moon, among other adventures. In the same vein, the recent sci-fi comedy movie *Iron Sky* (2012) staged vengeful Nazis living on the dark side of the moon, ready to re-conquer the Earth to establish a Fourth Reich.

The author of this book can only humbly report one strange case that a friend shared with him. Other independent sources do not confirm it. This friend's grandfather was among the first French aviators to fly over and bomb German soil even before ground troops set foot on it. He told my then 16-year-old friend that he saw aircraft or "space crafts" from "other worlds" on the German airfields, things he had never seen before in his entire life. He added that there were plenty of them, and that scared him tremendously since the Allied propaganda had promised to defeat the Third Reich quickly. He took many pictures of these "machines" and duly reported them in his flight book. He showed these pictures to my friend after the war sometime in the '70s.

When his grandfather died, nobody in the family ever found these pictures again. They were just gone. Could it have been the work of the French secret service?

Worth mentioning is his grandfather's fear in 1989 when he saw on television that the Berlin Wall had collapsed. The whole family rejoiced loudly at this progress of freedom, but he stayed still in front of the TV set, bleak and scared, just whispering aghast: "Oh no! ***It*** is coming back!"

Chapter 23

The Genocide

The first Allied soldiers who liberated the death camps had no words to describe what they had witnessed. The scenes they encountered were unlike anything in the annals of human suffering—a massive irruption of horror and barbaric practices that seemed to belong to a primitive era. Comparisons to the torments and tortures of the Inquisition in the Middle Ages inevitably came to mind, yet even that reference paled in comparison to the systematic and calculated horror of the Holocaust. The key distinction between this dark chapter of modern history and those earlier atrocities lay not only in the methods of killing but also in the magnitude of the evil: millions of innocent lives taken with chilling precision, creating an industrial-scale genocide that defied human understanding.

Most historians view the Holocaust as the inevitable outcome of the eugenic theories and anti-Semitic ideology at the heart of National Socialism. These ideas had been festering in Germany long before the Nazis rose to power, gaining momentum through pseudoscientific studies and racial purity propaganda. Undoubtedly, Nazi fanaticism and twisted ideological convictions provided much of the rationale for their actions. However, an intriguing question remains unanswered by mere political or ideological considerations: Why did the Germans prioritize train transports carrying Jews to extermination camps over their own military supply convoys during the final phase of the war? It was a time when the Third Reich desperately needed to mobilize all available resources to sustain the crumbling Eastern Front, yet they instead chose to divert those resources toward the continued extermination of millions of Jews and other "undesirables."

This inexplicable prioritization has led some to theorize that there may have been more behind the genocide. One of the first attempts to explore this theory came from Louis Pauwels and Jacques Bergier in their book *The Morning of the Magicians*. While their work is often criticized for being speculative and lacking in historical rigor, Pauwels and Bergier introduced an esoteric dimension to the motivations behind the genocide. According to their theories, members of the Thule Society believed that they could attain access to supernatural Powers through certain magical practices. These Powers, it was believed, could protect them from harm and anoint them as rulers of the world. In exchange for these gifts, the Powers demanded a form of tribute—human sacrifices.

Pauwels and Bergier claimed that, for some high-ranking Nazis, the genocide was not only about racial purity but also about fulfilling a form of covenant. The victims of the death camps became sacrificial offerings to gain favor from otherworldly forces, much like ancient civilizations that conducted rituals to appease the gods. They drew comparisons between the actions of the Nazis and those of the pre-Columbian Mayans, who sacrificed human lives to honor the sun and ensure the continuation of cosmic balance. The Nazis, according to this theory, sought to channel the sacrificial energy of their victims to harness divine power and secure victory—even when the war was clearly turning against them.

To the modern mind, such theories may sound absurd, but the fascination of many Nazi leaders with the occult is well documented. Heinrich Himmler was particularly interested in ancient rites and rituals that might help explain the perceived superiority of the Aryan race. The SS itself was organized as a pseudo-religious order, with initiations and symbols that evoked ancient Teutonic knighthood. Whether or not Himmler, or others in the Nazi hierarchy, believed that mass murder could serve a mystical purpose remains uncertain, but the existence of such theories underlines the esoteric undercurrents that might have been at work.

In 2003, David Brin and Scott Hampton published *The Life Eaters* through DC Comics, which offered an alternate history scenario that added another layer to the fantastical interpretation of the Holocaust. This sci-fi comic, belonging to the genre of uchronia (alternate history), envisioned a world in which the Nazis had successfully resurrected the ancient Norse gods to fight alongside them. According to Brin and Hampton's imaginative narrative, the Allied forces were annihilated on D-Day by the arrival of these resurrected gods. The story suggests that the millions of souls sacrificed by the Nazis in the death camps served to nourish these divine beings, giving them the strength to return to the mortal world. The concept was not only chilling in its imagery but also reflected a dark interpretation of historical events—the genocide as a grand occult ritual intended to invoke supernatural beings in the service of the Third Reich.

While *The Life Eaters* is, of course, a work of fiction, it draws on a long tradition of speculation about the Nazis' obsession with mythology and the occult. The idea that Hitler and his followers were engaged in something beyond conventional politics—something arcane and ritualistic—resonates with a need to explain the inexplicable. How could a cultured, advanced nation like Germany descend into such depravity and evil unless they were under some form of supernatural influence? This question has fueled countless conspiracy theories, some more plausible than others, and has even influenced popular culture.

The theories regarding the occult underpinnings of the Holocaust remain speculative, and there is no concrete historical evidence to suggest that the genocide was, in fact, a mass sacrificial ritual. However, the fascination with these ideas highlights a broader desire to find a deeper meaning behind one of the darkest events in human history.

It is important to differentiate between these theories and established historical facts. The Holocaust, at its core, was driven by a combination of ideological fanaticism, systemic racism, and political expediency. The decision to prioritize the extermination of Jews over the military needs of the German army can be explained by the ideological obsession of Hitler and his inner circle with achieving their vision of racial purity, even at the cost of military defeat.

Yet the persistence of these theories, and the way they continue to capture the imagination, suggests that there is something about the Holocaust that remains fundamentally incomprehensible. The scale of the suffering, the methodical nature of the killing, and the chilling efficiency of the machinery of death all contribute to a sense that there is something more—something darker—lurking beneath the surface of history. Whether or not the genocide had an esoteric component, the very existence of such theories reveals a deep-seated need to look beyond the rational, to see the Holocaust not only as a political or ideological event but as something more—a rupture in the fabric of human history that defies easy categorization or explanation.

Perhaps, in the end, the question of whether the genocide had an occult dimension is less important than what the existence of such a question tells us about ourselves. It tells us that, when faced with unimaginable evil, we seek explanations that transcend the ordinary. We reach for mythology, for magic, and for the supernatural—not because these explanations are necessarily true, but because they offer a way to frame the unthinkable. As we reflect on the Holocaust, we are forced to confront not only the historical facts but also the myths and mysteries that surround it.

Chapter 24

The Revival of Nazi Mysticism

The birth of a new religion needs a cosmogonical myth of creation, a God or a deified prophet, a clergy, a ritual, and followers who possess a strong enough holy Faith for proselytism. It is a much more subtle step, and it takes a much longer time to crystalize those ingredients in a successful alchemy than, for example, the more straightforward "Cargo Cults" that developed in some islands of the Pacific Ocean, particularly during WWII.

These religious ingredients were not all present at the time of Jesus, but they developed in the decades and even the few centuries after His earthly disappearance. The Catholic Church gave a structure and hierarchy through its bishops, formalizing the dogma and canon laws much later. This was especially the case in 325 AD, during the Council of Nicaea convened by the Roman emperor Constantine, who acted mainly for political reasons. This process could, of course, be demonstrated with all other religions or sectarian movements alike. Some even go so far as to state that a new religion is just a sect that has been proven to be historically successful.

National socialism was not regarded in its time as a religion, even by its most fanatic followers. The fact that Himmler did try to revive ancient pagan Germanic creeds was not linked to the ideological content of national socialism. On the contrary, the post-World War II period saw the emergence of different esoteric currents, claiming that there had been more to the Third Reich than what was studied by mainstream historians.

These esoteric currents are mainly linked to Savitri Devi and Miguel Serrano. However, there are also less famous authors from the far right and neo-pagan movements that contribute to what could be called the "semi-religious developments of Nazism." Let us add that the majority of neo-Pagans are not neo-Nazis nowadays.

Savitri Devi, who had French, Greek, and English blood, was born Maximiani Portasis. She studied chemistry as well as philosophy in France, where she obtained her PhD in Lyon. She can be rightfully regarded as the significant post-war thinker of "esoteric Hitlerism," aiming clearly at creating a religious movement from Nazism. According to her, Hitler's death in 1945 could be seen as martyrdom or a voluntary, Christ-like self-sacrifice. When the Russians entered Hitler's bunker, it was indeed empty, giving birth firstly to all kinds of escape speculations and secondly to a semi-religious myth.

This is how Savitri Devi writes in her book called *Pilgrimage*: "...National Socialism is infinitely more than a mere political creed; the fact is that it is a way of life, a faith in the fullest sense of the word – one could say a religion, however different it may at first appear, from every existing system thus labeled in current speech. Religions are not as easy to uproot as mere political creeds."

Savitri Devi, who advocated for Indian independence from British rule, somehow merged her esotericism with Hinduism. She considered Hitler to be Kalki, the tenth and final Avatar of Vishnu. For her, he was undoubtedly "the god-like Individual of our times, the Man against Time, the greatest European of all times."

Savitri Devi aka Maximiani Portasis

Hitler's death, in this way, could be seen as the beginning of a new religion, aiming at the spiritual and physical resurrection of the Aryans to rule the world again as the chosen people.

Miguel Serrano is the following most important figure who contributed to this religious trend of Nazism after 1945. He was a Chilean diplomat and had, therefore, many opportunities during his career to meet with people like Léon Degrelle, Otto Skorzeny, Hans-Ulrich Rudel, Marc Augier (*aka* "Saint-Loup"), Julius Evola, Wilhelm Landig, Herman Hesse, and Carl Jung.

While younger, in 1941, Miguel Serrano was initiated into an esoteric order in Santiago, Chile, practicing ritual magic linked with the Holy Masters who dwelled somewhere in Tibet. They were admirers of Hitler, whom they regarded as a bodhisattva incarnated on Earth to counter the evil effects of the Kali Yuga age.

Serrano's theories basically state that our material world is ruled by the Demiurge (Jehovah), who populated the planet with primitive beings doomed to be endlessly reincarnated, always at the same low level of existence. This purely gnostic and Manichaean view admitted their counterpart of good gods (the Hyperboreans of extraterrestrial origin), who tried their best to elevate the conscience and moral level of the Demiurge's poor humanoid creatures.

Miguel Serrano as a diplomat in India in 1957

Like the ancient astronaut theories, he lamented that the Nephilim (Fallen Angels), or renegade Hyperboreans, took advantage of their relationships with the Demiurge's human creatures to have sexual intercourse with them. This miscegenation diluted their light-bearing blood, emerging from the Black Sun and their divine energy power called Vril. To the Demiurge's delight, i.e., the tribal deity Jehovah of the Jews, this diminished the awareness of the divine on this planet, making it easier for him to control.

Serrano states thus, "There is nothing more mysterious than blood. Paracelsus considered it a condensation of light. I believe that the Aryan, Hyperborean blood is that but not the light of the Golden Sun, not of a galactic sun, but the light of the Black Sun, of the Green Ray." (See chapter on the Vril for explanations on the Green Color).

In this context, Hitler was seen as an emissary of the Higher Gods who vanished in his bunker in 1945 but who waited underground somewhere in Antarctica to emerge in the future with a fleet of UFOs, beat the Forces of Darkness (i.e., the Jews) and start a Fourth Reich.

Chapter 25

The Black Sun

History of religions, esotericism, and pseudo-sciences provide not a single aspect of the Black Sun but many. Beyond these differences, the question is whether one deals with different facets of the same theme, and if so, if they can be structured into a single one or if the Black Sun is just a generic name for unrelated phenomena. Nowadays, the Black Sun refers almost exclusively to a neo-Nazi symbol that can be found inlaid on the marble floor of the Wewelsburg castle in Germany.

The Egyptians

Alchemy, like Freemasonry, plunges its roots into Egyptian mythology. The solar cycle is probably the origin of one of the oldest myths that inspired the ancient Egyptians and mankind, as can be seen in the duality of Ra/Osiris. Ra dies after 12 hours of reign and resuscitates as Osiris during the next 12 hours, after which the latter dies to be reborn as Ra. Osiris stands for the Black Sun, and this natural cycle is tuned to the rhythm of our daily biological physiology and our souls reincarnating from one body to another.

Mesoamerican mythology

The Mesoamerican myths are shared by, among others, the Aztecs, the Mayans, the Mexicas, and the Toltecs. One prominent god familiar to these people is Quetzalcoatl, literally "feathered serpent," who incarnates one of the many mystical beliefs of the Black Sun in Central America. He would dive into the underworld with a blackened aura after his shining passage through the sky during the day.

The Aztecs compared the sun's passage into the underworld with a butterfly, an archetype for transformation and reincarnation. The only event when the Black Sun appeared during the day was a solar eclipse. He was then identified with the earth goddess Itzpapalotl, also called the "Obsidian Butterfly" (obsidian is a very dark volcanic stone), who would eat men during that exceptional cosmic event.

Whereas the Aztecs believed in five successive worlds corresponding to five suns, the fifth being ours, the Mexicas held the Black Sun for such an ancient sun that was the female origin of everything. It could be seen as a fecundity symbol coming from the womb of death, i.e., a metempsychosis or reincarnation principle.

The Alchemical Sol Niger

Alchemy, hermeticism, and gnosis tell us of the existence of two opposed Manichaean beliefs, corresponding, in our case, to two suns: an apparent material one (or "material gold") and a hidden one (or "philosophical gold"). The material sun of our planetary system, which consumes itself through a simple nuclear fusion based on hydrogen, could, as such, possibly be seen as a "Dark Sun," but still not a black one.

The strict alchemical principle of *Sol Niger* (literally: "Black Sun" in Latin) refers to the first stage of the *Magnum Opus* (i.e., the Great Work, at the end of which production of gold is obtained), also called the *Nigredo* or blackening phase.

From an operative viewpoint, the Magnum Opus greatly resembles the physical principle of nuclear fusion. Still, one should not neglect the speculative or mystical aspect of this alchemical process that may also refer to an internal spiritual transformation, popularized under others by Paulo Coelho in his book *The Alchemist*.

The Egyptian and historically unrelated Mesoamerican myths of the Black Sun, which refer to death, rebirth, and fecundity, suppose the underlying alchemical intermediary concept of *Putrefactio* (putrefaction or rotting in Latin).

A Black Sun can be seen in the colorful alchemical manuscript called *Splendor Solis* ("The Splendor of the Sun"), allegedly written in 1532/1535 by Solomon Trismosin, the spiritual father of Paracelsus. This sun is only partially visible and could be setting or rising in a desolated dried landscape of leafless trees, though remaining golden rays of light can be seen radiating weakly out of it. This Black Sun stands for putrefaction in alchemy. The accompanying text says that alchemy requires dissolution to obtain a black matter as the *nigredo* phase does.

Putrefaction, or death, is needed to give way to life and rebirth while the unconscious reconciles with the conscious. The culmination of this conciliation corresponds to the making of the Philosophical Stone, where the Putrefactio or Nigredo is the first part of the process. It is a phase where the pure should be separated from the impure, or as Carl Gustav Jung put it in psychoanalysis, to integrate the shadow into one's self, i.e., the dark side inside us.

Some alchemists also saw this as the association of the woman/moon and the man/sun into a Black Sun or a mystical wedding.

Salomon Trismosin - Splendor Solis, 1532-1535
at the Kupferstichkabinett of the Staatliche Museen zu Berlin

Theosophical Nemesis

In *The Secret Doctrine* (1888), Helena Blavatsky, founder of theosophy, mentioned a central invisible sun in the Milky Way. It would act as a center of attraction on our sun and an energetic source for the universe. Its energy was seen as a "creative light," though invisible, and which the Jews of the Cabala would call "the Black Light."

Interestingly enough, this matches precisely the modern astronomical theory of the existence of *Nemesis*, a hypothetical hard-to-detect brown dwarf star. The hypothesis was made in 1984 by paleontologists David Raup and Jack Sepkoski, who claimed that they had identified a statistical periodicity in extinction rates over the last 250 million years, which the regular passing of Nemesis could explain.

The Wewelsburg Sonnenrad

The castle of Wewelsburg was built in 1603 in North Rhine-Westphalia in Germany. In 1934, one year after the Nazi rise to power, Reichsführer Heinrich Himmler leased the castle for 100 years from the Paderborn district in order to make an ideological center for the Black Order of the SS.

The castle became an almost religious place where a handful of high-ranking SS, i.e., an elite within the elite, studied esotericism, runes, pagan lore, and racial theories. Himmler adapted the legend of King Arthur and his Knights to a new Grail mythology based on Germanic paganism.

In the center of the marbled floor of the *Gruppenführersaal* (SS Generals' Hall) on the first floor of the castle lies an inlaid dark green *Sonnenrad* ("sun wheel" in German). The axis of the *Sonnenrad* was made out of a pure golden disk that was supposed to become the center of the whole "Germanic world empire" from 1941 on. The design resembles that of Early Medieval Germanic brooches (*Zierscheiben*), possibly worn on Frankish and Alemannic women's belts. Its shape bears a solar significance, showing a twelve-spoke sun wheel looking like a decorative disk of the Merovingians that represented the passage of the visible sun through the months of the year. The design also evokes the Round Table of Arthurian legends, with each spoke of the sun wheel representing a 'knight' or an officer of the 'inner' SS.

It is most likely that this symbol was embedded during the Third Reich, but it is only after the Second World War that it was called *Die Schwarze Sonne* (Black Sun in German), though there is no evidence at all that Himmler's SS linked this symbol with that of the Black Sun. The very association between both seems to be a post-war esoteric interpretation that is still in use in certain scenes of neo-Nazism and Odinism.

Neo-Nazi Black Sun symbol

According to Jean-Michel Angebert (*Les mystiques du Soleil*, 1971), the swastika is actually the Black Sun, a principle of hidden energy in a multidimensional universe beyond the visible world. It is close to Iamblichus' philosophy based on gnosis. Without going so far, the sun wheel was possibly related to Germanic sun-based mysticism, which the SS propagated; the sun was interpreted as "the strongest and most visible expression of God."

Here, we find again the opposing traditional concepts of physical objects versus their spiritual expression: the marble Black Sun symbol from Wewelsburg vs. the inner light of a mystical universal creative energy. In the same way, the material cup of the Grail can be opposed to the alchemical properties of the beverage it holds, i.e., spiritual immortality. We can compare even further with the *Sol Invictus* ("Invincible Sun"), the official sun god of the later Roman Empire, who seems to have inspired Himmler's sun mysticism.

In 274 AD, the Roman emperor Aurelian made it an official cult alongside the traditional Roman cults. But like the inner light of the Black Sun or the immortality and mystical knowledge hidden in the Grail, *Sol Invictus* stood for a spiritual sun, a metaphysical concept only accessible to initiates, not just the physical sun visible to the exoteric crowds.

All these stories indeed added up to the myth that Castle Wewelsburg was an esoteric center, hiding not only rare historical artifacts (like the fake Celtic Cauldron of genuine pure gold recently found in the Chiem Lake in Germany) brought in by the Ahnenerbe but also the deepest spiritual secrets about the origins of the Nordic race.

Weisthor, Himmler's Rasputin

Karl Maria Wiligut, aka Weisthor, headed a Department for Pre and Early History that was created within the SS Race and Settlement Main Office (RuSHA). There, he developed plans for rebuilding Wewelsburg into a pseudo-religious center for the SS elite.

During the 1920s, he designed his own runic alphabet with mostly alternative meanings from the mainstream Futhark and wrote 38 verses called the *Halgarita Sprüche* with it.

He claimed to have memorized these verses as a child when taught by his father.

Werner von Bülow and Emil Rüdiger of the *Edda-Gesellschaft* (Edda Society) claimed some verses are connected with the

Black Sun, like verse number 27, which would be a 20,000-year-old "solar blessing" according to Willigut:

Sunur Saga santur toe
Syntir peri fuir Sprueh
Wilugoti Haga tharn
Halga fuir santur toe.

Karl Maria Wiligut aka Weisthor

Which translates, according to Werner von Bülow, more or less as follows, taking into account that this language probably exists only in Weisthor's brain:

"Legend tells that two Suns, two wholesome in change-rule UR and SUN, similar to the hourglass which turned upside down ever gives one of these the victory / The meaning of the divine errant wandering way/dross star in fire's sphere became in fire-tongue revealed to the Earth-I-course of the race of Paradise/god willing leaders lead to the weal through their care in the universal course, what is visible and soon hidden, whence they led the imagination of mankind / polar in change-play, from UR to SUN in sacrificial service of waxing and waning, in holy fire, Santur is ambiguously spent in sparks, but turns victorious to blessing."

These confused and almost incomprehensible verses are supposed to stress that *Santur* would be a burnt-out sun and power source for the Hyperboreans. These were purportedly the ancestors of Germanic tribes living at the North Pole when its climate was mild and its landscapes were green. Hyperborea had its capital city, Thule, and was once identified with Iceland. Furthermore, *Santur* allegedly still orbits in the vicinity of our planet as a Black Sun and sends powerful hidden energy. The latter recalls the Nemesis hypothesis and the invisible creative energy that a Black Sun is supposed to radiate.

The Vienna Circle

In the 4th district of Wieden in Vienna, Austria, ex-Waffen-SS Wilhelm Landig founded a group in 1950 called the Vienna Circle or, after him, the Landig Group. The group gathered for the first time at Landig's apartment and held a discussion on esoteric and völkisch (nationalist and racialist) mysticism. They revived and promoted the mythology of Hyperborea which was, as we saw, allegedly the home of the Aryans' ancestors in the Arctic.

According to Nicholas Goodrick-Clarke (*Black Sun, Esoteric Nazism and the Politics of Identity*, 2002), the Landig group invented the concept of the Black Sun that flourished in neo-Nazi groups during the 1990s. It was through Wilhelm Landig's own novels that this Nazi revival was made possible. He wrote a trilogy for this purpose: *Götzen gegen Thule, Rebellen für Thule,* and *Wolfszeit um Thule.*

Erich Halik, a prominent member of the Vienna Circle, was the first to link the esotericism of the inner SS elite with the Black Sun concept, but not yet to the Wewelsburg symbol. Landig called the Black Sun "a substitute Swastika and mystical source of energy, capable of regenerating the Aryan race." The visible sun would merely symbolize an invisible anti-sun: "Everything that human senses can comprehend is material, the shadow of the invisible spiritual light. The material fire is – seen in this way – also just the shadow of the spiritual fire."

Wilhelm Landig

Landig revived old völkisch pseudo-scientific theories about Atlantis, Hörbiger's Hollow Earth, and Aryan mysticism. In his trilogy, he locates in the Arctic the Aryan positive forces of the Black Sun, which, according to him, is represented by a disk that is not black but of a deep purple that will turn white when Germany eventually overcomes this titanic world struggle. Interestingly enough, Landig states that the Black Sun refers to the Babylonian religion, which in turn would come from the Aldebaran star, which "shines within us and gives us the power of understanding." For Landig, the Black Sun is the symbol for an esoteric order inside the SS, and it "shines above the Midnight Mountain an invisible light because it shines within." The Midnight Mountain seems to be present in the myths of different people throughout the globe, such as the Chinese and the Indians, the latter calling it Mount Meru.

Furthermore, Landig circulated stories about Nazi flying saucers assembled in an underground base in Antarctica (see Neuschwabenland expedition), from which US Admiral Byrd could not extirpate them.

More Post-War Nazi Fantasies

According to Nicholas Goodrick- Clarke, "In the early 1990s, the Austrians Norbert Jürgen Ratthofer and Ralf Ettl developed new Nazi UFO myths involving ancient Babylon, Vril energy and extraterrestrial civilizations in the solar system of Aldebaran. These colorful ideas are integral elements of a dualist Marcionite religion propagated by Ralf Ettl through his *Tempelhofgesellschaft* (Temple Society) in Vienna, identified as a secret successor to the historic Templars, who had absorbed Gnostic and heretical ideas in the Levant". Ratthofer and Ettl state in the DVD UFO – *Geheimnisse des Dritten Reichs* (1990) (UFO – Secrets of the Third Reich), "Within the SS the Thule Society created a separate secret organization called the 'Black Sun' with the 'Geheimnis Schwarze Sonne' as its logo."

In 1997 Peter Moon wrote *The Black Sun: Montauk's Nazi-Tibetan Connection,* in which he shows for the first time in Nazi occultism a picture of the "Signet of the Black Sun." This is allegedly the symbol of "the innermost secret society of Nazi Germany: the Black Sun."

In conclusion, the Black Sun can be seen as a multifaceted myth with an ancient background. However, it is not demonstrated that its various historical phases of development refer to the same concept. It is possible, though, to identify many common elements in these myths, which could contribute to unveiling parts of a unique and original truth.

The Black Sun seems to be an invisible counterpart of our visible sun, which can bestow its influence onto planets, things, and living beings. It hides from mortals, though keeping tuned with their very biological rhythms, but can be seen by souls in the Netherworld. Its alchemical and psycho-analytical meaning is that of a spiritual force able to lead a profound internal transformation prior to a total rebirth or reincarnation

Signet of the Black Sun

Nazis were after the spiritual secrets of the Nordic race, and they could have envisaged the Black Sun, at least in a very confidential inner circle of the SS, as a universal, pervasive force of creative energy that shines "from within." Some went so far as to state that this force would "allow souls to experience many levels of reality simultaneously."

The Black Sun of Tashi Lhunpo

(*Die Schwarze Sonne von Tashi Lhunpo*) is an occult Nazi thriller written in 1991 by Russel McCloud, a pen name for Stephan Mögle-Stadel. It tells of the assassinations of the president of the European Bank and a leading member of the UN Security Council, which are linked by a brand mark of the symbol of the Black Sun on the foreheads of the victims. This is the very first time that the symbol of the Sun Wheel, as found at the Wewelsburg castle, is linked with the Black Sun myth itself. If it contradicts the deep purple disk of Landig's trilogy, it evokes a universal creative energy source with its black circle and twelve radial sig runes. The only problem is that it seems to be pure fiction, Stephan Mögle-Stadel being just a journalist enjoying writing a thriller.

Nonetheless, the neo-Nazi scene adopted the Wewelsburg Sonnenrad as the one and only true symbol of the Black Sun and a legal substitute for the swastika, which is forbidden in many European countries.

Chapter 26

The Vril

The Vril, as well as the secret society bearing its name, is now a traditional stopover in the meanders of so-called Nazi esotericism. Compared to the Black Sun, the Vril's very existence is controversial, and sometimes, we shall have to depart from historically verifiable facts to enter a twilight zone between myth and reality. But how unreal are the myths?

In the Beginning, Was a Sci-Fi Novel

Many sects begin with a single man's sayings or visions, whereas others are based on a holy book or even a novel. This is the case of Scientology, but it could be applied to some extent to other very successful religions. The Vril was first mentioned in a book entitled *The Coming Race*, written by Sir Edward Bulwer-Lytton in 1871. Though the term "science fiction" did not exist then, it would fit well in this book and in Jules Verne's. He also wrote *Zanoni*, an occult fiction, and the famous *Last Days of Pompeii*.

The plot centers on a traveler who lost his way in an old mine in Great Britain, only to find himself the guest of an antediluvian underground race called the Vril-ya. Neither gods nor angels, however, look far superior to humans by their height, intelligence, cold wisdom, and supernatural powers like telepathy. They harness an "all-permeating" fluid called Vril. Through training their will, they can master this universal, invisible, creative energy that can heal, transform, or destroy, besides acting as a fuel for transportation devices and lighting the underground. The latter was of a light green luminescence.

Sir Edward Bulwer-Lytton

Zee, his host's daughter, teaches the hero and narrator the most accessible history of the Vril-ya. He learns that when the underground caves are insufficient for their breeding, the Vril-ya will have to conquer the surface world, destroying mankind if necessary. Vril is indeed so powerful that a Vril-ya child could reduce a city of tens of millions of inhabitants to ashes in a matter of seconds.

The narrator studies the Vril-ya language and draws the conclusion that they are "descended from the same ancestors as the great Aryan family, from which in varied streams has flowed the dominant civilization of the world."

Somehow, the Vril-ya have much in common with Lovecraft's Unknown Superiors: telepathy, mastery of unknown forces, and an antediluvian ancestry.

Black Sun & Alchemy

One ought to be cautious with all that refers to esotericism since one fake myth reinforces the other, especially on the Internet. Nonetheless, the idea exists that Bulwer-Lytton only based his novel on more ancient myths and archetypes, which were popular among Middle Ages alchemists. The life force underlying the Vril has indeed been known since antiquity as Prana, Chi, Ojas, Astral Light, Odic Force, and Orgone. Some advocates of the Hollow Earth Theory have even said, more recently, that Vril came from the Black Sun, a hidden force that would be an irradiating *Prima Materia* ("primordial matter" in Latin) at the center of our planet.

Green is the Color of the Vril

The green light that illuminates the Vril-ya's underworld reminds of many other occurrences of that color: Goethe's tale The Green Snake and the Beautiful Lily; the Holy Grail that could be an emerald fallen from Lucifer's forehead; Greenland, named in the 10th century by Erik the Red, in remembrance of the Primordial Earth, though 60 percent of the island was by then already covered by white ice; certain Egyptologists saw Osiris as a green irradiating god; the Mesoamerican Quetzalcoatl Great Priest drew their might from an enormous magical emerald, and the god himself was green; the famous Emerald Tablet (Tabula smaragdina) of the hermetic tradition of the alchemists; eventually, some green lunar stones would possess a "levitation" power enabling witches to fly in old Scottish lore or, hidden under cathedrals, would have prevented bombs from falling onto them during WWII in Germany.

Quetzalcoatl

Let us give special mention to the Order of the Green Dragon and the Monk with the Green Gloves.

The Order of the Green Dragon was a Japanese secret (political/mystical) society dedicated to mastering the human body, which in turn permitted access to a "great power." Higher initiates were required to be able to germinate a seed by telekinesis.

While a military attaché in Tokyo before WWI, Karl Haushofer would have been one of just three Westerner members of the Order. Haushofer was one of the founders of geopolitics (the theory of *Lebensraum* or vital space) and allegedly also a member of the Vril Society. He never was a member of the Nazi Party and was even married to a Jewish woman despite many contrary assertions in neo-Nazi esoteric literature.

The Vril Society profess to have sent expeditions to Tibet before WWII and as late as 1942 to meet the Bon Pö monks of Agarthi. In the '20s, Tibetan monks formed the Society of Green Men in Berlin and Munich. Their High Priest was a man called the Monk with the Green Gloves. Hitler would have visited him for his clairvoyant gifts.

The Society of Green Men, helped by the Order of the Green Dragon, allegedly helped the Nazis to try to turn Aryans into God- Men. Pauwels and Bergier, in their *Morning of the Magicians*, a very unreliable source but the only one on this subject, report that during the fall of Berlin, the Russians found many dead bodies of Asians in German uniforms who apparently ritually committed suicide.

According to the same source, Haushofer would have committed the same kind of suicide, except that this is historically untrue. Historian H. A. Jacobsen proved that all that was written in *The Morning of the Magicians* about him, the Thule Society, and the Vril Society is simply fiction.

The Vril Society

Louis Jacolliot (1837–1890) was a French consul in Calcutta, India, when he wrote *Les fils de Dieu* (1873) and *Les Traditions indo-européennes* (1876). Both books stressed the existence of the Vril, which appeared a bit earlier in Bulwer-Lytton's novel *The Coming Race* (1871). Jacolliot is supposed to have met the Vril among the Jains in Mysore and Gujarat, the country where he lived as a diplomat and judge.

Madame Helena Blavatsky, the founder of theosophy, was also impressed by Bulwer-Lytton's book. She found confirmation of the racial aspects of her theories concerning the origin of mankind, which she wrote in her books *Isis Unveiled* (1877) and again in *The Secret Doctrine* (1888). The physical and spiritual superiority of the white race was later mixed with anti-

Semitism, and the first studies of the Indo-European peoples by the German nationalists gave thus birth to ariosophy (Aryan + theosophy). It mainly was the works of Guido von List and Jörg Lanz von Liebenfels.

Both Louis Jacolliot and Madame Blavatsky supported Bulwer-Lytton's Vril myth so well that many contemporaries actually believed in the existence of this green force.

According to Joscelyn Godwin (*Arktos: The Polar Myth in Science, Symbolism, and Nazi Survival*), the only primary source of information on the Vril Society is Willy Ley.

Willy Ley was a German rocket engineer who fled Nazi Germany in 1933. In 1947, he published "Pseudoscience in Naziland" in *Astounding Science Fiction*. He explained that the Nazis did obtain many technical successes because they systematically tried every option possible in all scientific fields and beyond. This included the pseudo-sciences of the Hollow Earth, the *Welteislehre* (The World Ice Theory), and even magic at the fringe. Among these weird theories, there really existed, according to Ley, a group interested in Vril:

"The next group was literally founded upon a novel. That group, which I think called itself *Wahrheitsgesellschaft* (Society for Truth) and which was more or less localized in Berlin, devoted its spare time looking for Vril. Yes, their convictions were founded upon Bulwer-Lytton's *The Corning Race*. They knew that the book was fiction; Bulwer-Lytton had used that device to be able to tell the truth about this "power." The underground humanity was nonsense; Vril was not. It enabled the British, who kept it a State secret, to amass their colonial empire. Indeed, the Romans had it enclosed in small metal balls, which guarded their homes and were referred to as *Lares*. For reasons I failed to penetrate, the secret of Vril could be found by contemplating the structure of an apple sliced in halves.

No, I am not joking. That is what I was told with great solemnity and secrecy. Such a group actually existed. They even published the first issue of a magazine to proclaim their credo (I wish I had kept some of these things, but I had enough books to smuggle out as it was).

(Left to right) Heinz Haber, Wernher von Braun, Willy Ley

Professor Nicholas Goodrick-Clarke (*Black Sun: Aryan Cults, Esoteric Nazism, and the Politics of Identity*, 2002) tells a different and more probable account based on the findings of Dr. Peter Bahn in his 1996 essay, *Das Geheimnis der Vril-Energie* (The Secret of the Vril energy): "The reality of the Vril Society was a good deal less impressive. Its formal name was Reichsarbeitsgemeinschaft "Das Kommende Deutschland" (Reich Working Group 'The Coming Germany'); one of the hundreds of little occult societies in Weimer Germany, it was sponsored by the astrological publisher Wilhelm Becker. The group put out a magazine, which apparently folded after one issue.

In 1930, it also published two pamphlets, *Vril: Die kosmische Urkraft* (Vril: The Primal Cosmic Power) and *Weltdynamismus* (World Dynamism), claiming to reveal the secrets of Atlantean free energy technology. A section of the latter pamphlet shows a bisected apple as a symbol of the free energy field surrounding the earth. While this confirms Ley's account, it does nothing to back up the extravagant claims made for the Vril Society's activities and influence by later writers."

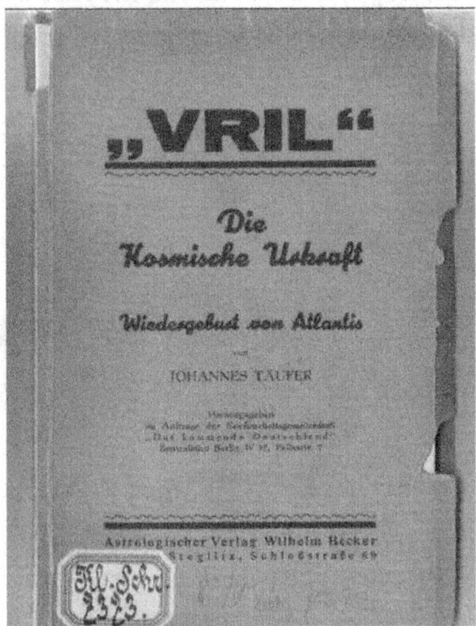

Vril: The Primal Cosmic Power

Last but not least, some went so far as to claim that the Nazis wanted to change Nordic Germans into a super-race, to become equals with the supermen inside the earth. They would have tried to use different meditation methods to obtain this transformation. These methods were allegedly based on tantric Buddhism and Tibetan Bon Pö pre-Buddhist "black" shamanism, as well as on Ignatius Loyola's *Spiritual exercises*.

The existence of a Vril Society was mentioned for the first time as such in 1960 by Bergier and Pauwels in their best-seller. It looked like other secret societies that pretended to have existed then, like the Thule Society and the Golden Dawn. They quote the excerpt of "Pseudoscience in Naziland," where Dr. Willy Ley wrote about that strange society and linked it to the ritual suicide of the Tibetan monks in Berlin's final days. For the latter, the most likely is that they were Asians from "liberated"

Soviet republics enrolled in the Nazi struggle against communism. There were also well-known similar cases of Indians serving in German uniforms on the Atlantic Wall bunkers in France.

Van Helsing's Myths of the '90s

With German author Jan van Helsing, aka Jan Udo Holey, the Vril myth reaches its climax, but indeed not the historical truth. Van Helsing wrote about modern secret Nazi UFO bases in Antarctica as the achievement of a prolonged underground activity that began in the '20s among members of secret societies.

Maria Orsitsch (*Marija Oršić* in Croatian) was allegedly a powerful medium and member of the Vril Society. Her father was a Croatian immigrant from Zagreb, while her mother was Austrian.

She would have met in 1917 with Karl Haushofer, Baron Rudolf von Sebottendorf (Thule Society), and Prelate Gernot of the secret *Societas Templi Marcioni* (The Inheritors of the Knights Templar) in the Schopenhauer café in Vienna. They would have been admirers of the Hermetic Order of the Golden Dawn and disciples of secret Asian lodges, hence the presence of Tibetan monks in Berlin and Munich. As we already saw, this is pure fantasy, at least as far as Karl Haushofer is concerned.

They studied secret texts of the Knights Templar and were linked to the secret fraternity *Die Herren vom schwarzen Stein* ("The Lords of the Black Stone"), the existence of which is to be found nowhere else.

Maria would have gotten acquainted in Munich with members of the Thule Gesellschaft and started her own female medium group initially called *Alldeutsche Gesellschaft für Metaphysik*.

They all had long ponytails that they believed acted as cosmic antennas, to receive alien communication.

In 1919, a few members of all these secret societies met at a small alpine lodge close to Berchtesgaden. There, Maria Oršić and another medium named Sigrun claimed to have received telepathic transmissions from Aldebaran star in a secret Templar writing containing technical blueprints for the construction of flying machines. The language used to code the message would have been nothing less exotic than ancient Sumerian, "that sounded like German" (*sic*).

Maria Orsitsch aka Marija Oršić

What follows is a series of different Vril UFOs (Vril-7, Haunebu I, II, etc.) and the project to reach Aldebaran one day by traveling with these. Of course, a multi-dimensional channel, independent of Einstein's Relativity equations, would lead them to the star of their dreams.

Maria Oršić disappeared in 1945, leaving behind her a letter to all the members of her lodge, where she wrote: "Niemand bleibt hier" (no one stays here). It is speculated that she and her friends escaped to Aldebaran and, if not, at least to Nazi Antarctica, which is much closer indeed!

One can safely say that Vril is at least a controversial subject. It is not necessary to make it ridiculous by inventing unsubstantiated stories with no references and no hard evidence to support them. Truth seekers do respect good research work and dismiss parrots that echo rumors and urban legends. All genuine myths hide some truth and deserve to be treated seriously and with respect.

Vril is a word that Bulwer-Lytton probably invented in his novel since it is the first time it is mentioned. Nonetheless, the concept of a hidden universal creative force that can be harnessed and mastered is not new. It has predecessors in the history of religions, philosophy, and occultism and could possibly be newly interpreted in the light of quantum physics.

The Vril Society was likely the group called *Reichsarbeitsgemeinschaft "Das Kommende Deutschland."* It indeed looked after the Vril and its mastery. It has, however, no proven links with the Thule Society, which, based on known evidence, did exist but had already disappeared by then. Karl Haushofer was not a member of the latter, neither was Rudolf Hess, and they most probably never reached the attention of leading Nazis. It is true, though, at least regarding the Thule Society, that they were deeply involved in fighting the short-lived Soviet Republic of Bavaria after WWI.

On the other hand, the legend of Maria Oršić is based on nothing since not even her birth certificate could be found. Of course, some will argue that the people of Aldebaran took it with them or, as can be read in fantasy books pretending to hold some truth, that the Vril members erased all tracks behind them for "security purposes."

Epilogue

One may wonder why books, movies, and even video games about WWII are still so successful, especially when they tackle Nazism and its dark side. Perhaps this fascination endures because WWII was the last historical event of truly global proportions, a clash of ideologies and civilizations that fundamentally shaped the world we live in today. As we now reside in what some call the "End of History," a postmodern world characterized by the dominance of liberal democracies and the global spread of market economies, the allure of the past is amplified. The post-1945 world is largely controlled by the notion of the "Empire of the Good," a belief in moral superiority, and an emphasis on individual rights and material prosperity. In this sanitized modern reality, evil, conflict, and ideological struggle are relics of an era when the foundations of our civilization were at stake. These elements are no longer as visible or as threatening, which is why their portrayal in popular culture is even more captivating.

In this perspective, occult Nazism has become a symbol of the "evil of Evil," with Hitler embodying a Lucifer-like figure.

Postmodern man craves the thrill of history but in a secure, detached manner—one without real danger or consequences. We want to feel rebellious, to fight against a malevolent force, all while being supported by the law, government, "well-meaning" NGOs, and new moral institutions. This desire has given rise to a new kind of hero: a "Rebel Without a Real Cause," who battles the ghosts of the past without ever putting anything at stake. Modern individuals like to believe they are unique while, in reality, they are part of a collective of billions, all playing at heroism without any real cost.

The allure of occult Nazism stems from these very feelings. No event since WWII has matched its magnitude in terms of historical impact. Conflicts like the Vietnam War or the Korean War had tragic human costs, but they did not possess the world-altering stakes of the Second World War. Instead, they were proxy wars, expressions of the geopolitical struggle between the United States and the Soviet Union. They were meant to draw red lines, to establish boundaries between the Western bloc and the communist world, rather than being decisive battles for the future of humanity. In essence, they were more akin to backyard quarrels—tragic, yes, but not transformative in the same way.

As the specter of Evil vanishes, we feel a growing sense of purposelessness, as it was the very fuel that drove the narrative of history. Without that "necessary other" to oppose, modern life can feel devoid of the higher meaning that comes from struggle and sacrifice. To fill this void, modern man replaces genuine evil with "mock enemies" and manufactured crises. Consider, for example, the portrayal of Saddam Hussein as a new Hitler in the lead-up to the Iraq War, complete with fabricated claims of weapons of mass destruction. We like to be frightened, but only when we know that a Hollywood-style happy ending is assured.

This is why occult Nazism has transformed into a myth after WWII. All the elements are present: villains, secret societies, magic, esotericism, and the clash of ideologies—all taking place in a world that was being reshaped. The imagery of Nazis conducting occult rituals or seeking supernatural power taps into our need to understand them as something more than human. If their actions were the result of an unearthly Evil, then perhaps we can better comprehend the depths of their depravity.

That being said, many authors have capitalized on this demand, identifying a lucrative gap in the market. They wrote sensational accounts, often blurring the lines between fact and fiction. Some were content to peddle pure fantasy, while others took a more insidious route, presenting fiction as fact to the extent that their stories birthed urban legends and new myths that continue to thrive on the Internet. These myths, often passed on like rumors, are built upon each other, adding increasingly fantastic details over time. Some began as jokes, others as commercial tricks to attract readers, but the result has been a dense web of misinformation, which, although entertaining, has little basis in truth.

In the realm of genuine history, there was indeed an element of Nazi occultism, as well as numerous little-known oddities linked to the Third Reich. Heinrich Himmler, the head of the SS, was notoriously obsessed with occult practices and ancient rites. He spearheaded the establishment of the Ahnenerbe, an organization dedicated to researching Aryan heritage and mystical traditions. The SS saw itself as a modern-day knightly order, and its rituals were steeped in symbolism that evoked ancient Teutonic traditions. The fascination of the Nazi elite with mysticism and esotericism also extended to expeditions in search of lost knowledge, such as the infamous 1938-1939 SS expedition to Tibet. These are real, verifiable events that demonstrate a strange confluence of pseudo-historical mythology and political ideology.

These historical oddities are interesting and testify to a time when reality itself seemed to stretch to its limits, a period that left contemporaries and later generations in awe. The genuine history of the Third Reich includes many bizarre aspects that reflect the irrational, quasi-religious beliefs held by certain members of the Nazi leadership.

The fascination with occult Nazism and the persistent myths it inspires reflect our collective struggle to make sense of an era marked by unparalleled evil. The need to mythologize the Nazis as something more than human—whether demonic or occult—is an attempt to rationalize actions that seem to defy explanation. In the end, it is not the fantasies that matter, but the lessons we draw from the real history of those dark times. And perhaps, in seeking to understand the true nature of this evil, we come to a deeper understanding of ourselves and our own potential for both darkness and light.

One may wonder why books, movies, and even video games about WWII are still so successful, especially when they tackle Nazism and its dark side. Maybe because WWII was the last historical event of global proportion, and we presently live after the End of History in a postmodern world controlled by the Empire of the Good. Evil, negation, fights, and ideologies were only necessary when the foundations of our civilization were at stake. It is no longer the case since 1945. Everywhere in the world, we see people aspiring to achieve the same levels of material comfort based on the same moral and economic individualistic values. "Evil" is no longer a real threat, but one is asked to believe in its present existence more than ever.

In this perspective, occult Nazism is the evil of Evil, and Hitler incarnates Lucifer. Postmodern man wants the thrill of history but in a sanitized version, without the risk and the pain. He wants to be a "rebel" supported by the law, the government, "well-meaning" NGOs, and new moral institutions. *A Rebel Without a Real Cause*, fighting long-gone ghosts. In other words, a modern man pretends to be unique while his billions of clones play the hero at no cost, never putting their lives at stake as they insistently pretend to.

The attraction of occult Nazism comes from these feelings because no more significant event than WWII ever happened in our post-historical world. Most small wars after WWII, like the Vietnam War, did have casualties, but they were not meant to change the world. They were meant to draw a red line between the West and the communist empire to make them understand that it should not be trespassed. It was more of a backyard quarrel. No less, no more.

The more Evil vanishes away, the more we feel purposeless since it was the very fuel of history, that necessary dialectical "other" we could fight with bravery. Modern man replaces evil with "mock enemies" and fake events, such as comparing Saddam Hussein to Hitler by making up stories of weapons of mass destruction. We like to be scared, knowing that a Hollywood happy ending always waits for us around the corner.

This is the reason why occult Nazism became a myth after WWII. All the ingredients are there: bad guys, witches, magic, esotericism, and the fight against irreconcilable ideologies in an environment of a new history in the making.

That being said, many authors identified a juicy gap in the market and began to write nonsense, or, far more dishonest, to make up stories that would even give birth to urban legends and new myths on the Internet. Spreading like rumors, each myth relied on the previous one and added new fantastic elements. Some are jokes, some are commercial traps, but none is true.

As far as history is concerned, there was a genuine Nazi occultism and many other unknown odd facts that were related to the Third Reich. We dealt with them in this book because they are interesting enough and bear a deep meaning that does not require making things up or creating a fantasy. They are in itself a testimony of no ordinary times. They are, like Nazism, a breach in the fabric of history that left its contemporaries in awe.

PICTURE CREDITS

Page	Attribution	License
18	Bundesarchiv, Bild 183-1997-0923-500/Hubmann, Hanns	CC-BY-SA 3.0
19	African serving in the Free Arabian legion	PD
20	Bundesarchiv, Bild 101I-177-1465-16 / Schlickum /	CC-BY-SA 3.0
21	Bundesarchiv, Bild 183-J16695	CC-BY-SA 3.0
22	Bundesarchiv, Bild 101III-Mielke-036-23 / Mielke	CC-BY-SA 3.0
24	Bundesarchiv, Bild 146-1973-010-11	CC-BY-SA 3.0 DE
25	Bundesarchiv, Bild 146-1969-062A-56	CC-BY-SA 3.0
30	Lake Toplitz	PD
36	Werwolf insignia on pennant	PD
37	SS General Prützmann meets with Himmler	PD
42	Honza Groh	PD
43	Bundesarchiv, Bild 146-1991-061-17	CC-BY-SA 3.0
44	Przykuta	CC-BY-SA 3.0
46	Jakub Hałun	CC-BY-SA 4.0
48	Archiv der Gedenkstätte Buchenwald	FU/UN
48	Amber Room	PD
52	Esadof modifiziert von birkho	CC-BY-SA 4.0
55	Type XXI U-boats in Bergen, Norway	CC-BY-SA 4.0
56	Panzer VIII Maus with crew members	PD
57	Nick-D	CC-BY-SA 3.0
58	V2 Rocket	PD
59	Horten Ho 229	PD
61	Flettner Fl 282	PD
62	Fieseler Fi 103R	PD
63	Messerschmitt Me 163	PD
64	Me 262 at the National Museum in Dayton	PD
66	Dora gun	PD
68	Pervitin	PD
72	Dr. Theodor Morell	FU/UN
75	Mugshots from Göring's detention	PD
78	Experimental nuclear pile at Haigerloch	PD
79	Vemork hydroelectric power plant	PD
82	German members of the Von Braun group	PD
83	Bumper V-2 Launch	CC BY-NC 2.0
88	Emblem of the Thule Society	FU/UN
92	The Hollow Earth Map	FU/UN
96	Hanns Hörbiger	PD
100	Peter Kiehlmann Collection	FU/UN

102	Official insignia of the 1938-1939 expedition	PD
106	Official insignia of the Ahnenerbe	PD
108	Bundesarchiv, Bild 135-KA-10-072	CC-BY-SA 3.0
110	Mhwater	PD
114	Tbachner	CC-BY-SA 3.0
115	Gruppenführer hall	FU/UN
116	Dirk Vorderstraße	CC BY 2.0
118	Chronicle of Schilling of Lucerne (1513)	PD
120	Files from the Witch Special Operation	FU/UN
121	Alleged SS file about a Devil's Pact	FU/UN
129	Wotan aka Odin, the Norse God	PD
136	Bundesarchiv, Bild 101I-295-1561-09 /Müller, Karl	CC-BY-SA 3.0 DE
137	Hermann Rauschning	PD
142	Bundesarchiv, Bild 183-S62600	CC-BY-SA 3.0 DE
144	Bundesarchiv, Bild 183-V04744	CC-BY-SA 3.0 DE
145	Hitler's alleged remains	FU/UN
148	Saint-Loup in 1942 in Smolensk	FU/UN
149	The Zillertal around 1898	PD
150	Otto Rahn	FU/UN
154	WeskerX	PD
155	Cooling Tower in Siechnice, Poland	PD
157	Alleged picture of a Schallkanone	PD
158	Real Repulsine device	PD
158	Repulsine with a Luftwaffe cross	PD
159	Rare picture of Foo Fighters	PD
160	Adamski street lamp debunked UFO	PD
161	Rudolf Schriever's flying device	PD
161	Prototype of the Sack AS-6	PD
173	Savitri Devi aka Maximiani Portasis	FU/UN
174	Miguel Serrano as a diplomat	PD
180	Salomon Trismosin - Splendor Solis	PD
182	Neo-Nazi Black Sun symbol	CCBY-SA2.0DE
184	Karl Maria Wiligut	FU/UN
186	Wilhelm Landig	FU/UN
188	Signet of the Black Sun	FU/UN
192	Sir Edward Bulwer-Lytton	FU/UN
194	Quetzalcoatl	FU/UN
197	H. Haber, Wernher von Braun, Willy Ley	PD
198	Vril: The Primal Cosmic Power	FU/UN
200	Maria Orsitsch	FU/UN

CC BY-SA 2.0 DE (from Wikipedia): This file is licensed under the Creative Commons Attribution-Share Alike 2.0 Germany license. (http://creativecommons.org/licenses/by-sa/2.0/de/deed.en)

CC BY-SA 3.0 DE (from Wikipedia): This file is licensed under the Creative Commons Attribution-Share Alike 3.0 Germany license. (http://creativecommons.org/licenses/by-sa/3.0/de/deed.en)

CC BY-SA 3.0 (from Wikipedia): This file is licensed under the Creative Commons Attribution-Share Alike 3.0 Unported license. (http://creativecommons.org/licenses/by-sa/3.0/deed.en)

FU/UN: Fair Use or Unknown copyright holder if any.

PD: Public domain

Made in the USA

Made in the USA
Middletown, DE
13 February 2025